Charlton Heston

THE EPIC PRESENCE

BRUCE CROWTHER

COLUMBUS BOOKS
LONDON

ACKNOWLEDGEMENTS

I gratefully acknowledge the help of Jonathan Hartman, Geoff
Napthine, Armin Otte, Dave and Wendy Smith and Dave Tuck
during preparation of this book. As always, the staffs of various
libraries have proved efficient and invaluable, in particular those at
the British Film Institute, the British Library at Colindale, the
Brynmor Jones Library at the University of Hull and the Central
Public Library of Hull.

B.C.

PICTURE CREDITS

Some of the illustrations in this book come from stills issued to
publicize films made or distributed by the following companies:
Allied Artists, American International, Columbia, EMI, MGM,
Paramount, Rank, TCF, United Artists, Universal, Warner.

Pictures are reproduced courtesy of Napthine-Walsh Collections.

Although efforts have been made to trace present copyright holders
of photographs, the publishers apologize in advance for any
unintentional omission or neglect and will be pleased to insert the
appropriate acknowledgement to companies or individuals in any
subsequent edition of this book.

Copyright © 1986 Bruce Crowther

First published in Great Britain in 1986 by
COLUMBUS BOOKS
Devonshire House, 29 Elmfield Road, Bromley,
Kent BR1 1LT

Designed by Fred Price

British Library Cataloguing in Publication Data
Crowther, Bruce
    Charlton Heston: the epic presence.
    1. Heston, Charlton   2. Moving-picture
    actors and actresses — United States —
    Biography
    I. Title
    792'.028'0924   PN2287.H47
    ISBN 0–86287–287–1

Phototypeset by Falcon Graphic Art Ltd
Wallington, Surrey
Printed and bound by
R.J. Acford, Chichester, Sussex

Opposite title: Charlton Heston, in the Egyptian desert for the 1980 film The Awakening.

CONTENTS

INTRODUCTION

Countless screen actors have been stereotyped as a result of Holly-wood's often unimaginative handling of their careers. Even those actors who have been able to exercise some personal control have still encountered problems when financial backing has been refused for anything that suggested a shift away from a tried, if often grossly over-used, formula. There are also actors who have been pigeon-holed not by Hollywood but by critics and public and within this group is a tiny handful whose stereotyping is entirely unjustified. Among these actors, Charlton Heston is undoubtedly the most visible example.

Heston's categorization as an 'epic actor' flies in the face of fact. In his entire film career, less than one in ten of his roles, now approaching 60, has been in films which can be truly termed epics. Even more misleading in its implications is the suggestion that he is a 'biblical' actor, but this is even less accurate as he has played only two such roles. Why should such misjudgements have occurred? It may well be that they are a side effect of the air of seriousness which enshrouds him, the physical dignity and the impression of probity, of high ideals and principles that his presence conveys. There is also his studious approach to the roles he plays, even when the films themselves have sometimes proved unworthy of such care.

Heston's work, his attitude towards it and his outwardly solemn public mien all contribute towards the mistaken view that he is a gloomy man forever playing larger-than-life roles in massive, lumber-ing movies.

His performances have rarely garnered unqualified critical acclaim, perhaps as a result of his unjustified 'epics-only' label, for epics are a

genre which few critics are able to take seriously, let alone accommo-
date in a favourable manner. The fact that he, a mere actor, takes
himself and his work seriously may also be resented by the many critics
who take themselves far too seriously for their own good. As a result,
these critics have bogged themselves, and film criticism, down in a
morass of intellectual judgements within which the actor is simultaneously the least considered and most reviled contributor.

The public's attitude towards Heston is somewhat ambivalent.
Undoubtedly his presence helps at the box-office and, as is demonstrated whenever he appears in public, people clearly like and admire
him. Yet, unlike many actors whom the critics have taken against (until
they reached almost mythic proportions), Heston has never attained
the same kind of popular following accorded to, say, John Wayne or
Clint Eastwood or Robert Redford. The cause of this may well be, in
part, the roles with which the public most closely associates him and
also his air of aloofness, an air which is rooted not in self-esteem but in
a surprising shyness and a deep desire to maintain his privacy.

Such characteristics, which reflect the public's ambivalence, appear
in both his professional and his personal life, where they occasionally
conflict and contrast. As an actor he only rarely reveals the man inside,
yet his seeming reluctance, or inability, to put his emotions on public
display contrasts with his decision to publish his diaries, wherein some
entries reveal more of himself than those actors who have written
'tell-all' biographies. His early ground-breaking contractual arrangements in Hollywood, which allowed many of the actors who followed to
take control of their careers, contrasts with his latterday association
with the film world's sometimes moribund establishment. His recent
bitter public battles with the leadership of the Screen Actors' Guild
over responses to the rebels in El Salvador contrasts with his alignment
with the Civil Rights movement in the years before it became a
fashionable issue.

Then there is his scandal-free private life and his marriage of more
than 40 years with only rare hints of discord, all of which contrasts
startlingly with most film-world relationships.

Heston also differs from many other screen actors in that he has
never lost either his love for or his dedication to the legitimate theatre.

This continuing contact with the theatre has added to the difficulties
some have in assessing him as a screen actor, especially as he has
consistently displayed a love for the great and most demanding stage
roles in both Shakespeare and the modern American classics. Such an
attitude from an actor sits uncomfortably with those who prefer to keep
movie stars in categories, even to the extent of painstakingly fabricating

the categories themselves. Heston's regular return visits to the stage are often made at personal financial cost and this determination to act in the theatre – which he describes as the renewal of his citizenship – is sometimes achieved by openly taking movie roles just for the money. Actions such as this, which may well account for the fact that he has appeared in some remarkable duds, can hardly have endeared him to those fellow actors who take the money for somewhat less lofty reasons.

Charlton Heston is, then, a man of contrasts and conflicting currents, all of which make him much more interesting both as an actor and as a man than a cursory view of his life and career might suggest.

Now that he has returned to television, which is where he first attracted national attention during the heady days of live TV drama in America, he is more than ever in the public eye. Because his return is in the central role in *Dynasty II: The Colbys*, the acme of American soap opera, he is inevitably attracting a great deal of that negative critical response that has dogged him in the past.

This is, therefore, an ideal moment to re-examine an acting career which is now entering its fifth decade and to discover how and why he has prospered when so many have fallen by the way, and also to explore the reasons why he has simultaneously failed to gain the level of critical approval often granted to actors of considerably less merit and distinction.

CHAPTER
One

'Yes, but do we need another Burt Lancaster?'
Hal Wallis

Charlton Heston was born in Evanston, Illinois on 4 October 1923, the eldest son of Russell and Lilla Carter, whose maiden name was Charlton. His parents divorced when he was nine and when Lilla remarried she and her children took the surname of her new husband, Chester Heston.

Evanston, a town of some 80,000 inhabitants, is located on the shores of Lake Michigan, but Charlton Heston's early childhood was spent upstate in the tiny community of St Helen. This is in an isolated forested region, a perfect place in which a small boy could grow up, and he would always look back on these years as a time of idyllic happiness. The size of St Helen meant that there were few other children around, but this absence of companionship seems to have troubled him little if at all. He had a younger brother and sister, Alan and Lilla, but there were still only 13 pupils with whom to share his education in the one-room St Helen school.

Even this early in life he displayed an interest in acting which far exceeded the imaginative play-acting of most small boys. In this he was doubtless encouraged by his mother's uncle, Percy Charlton, an actor of some note. Like many children, young Charlton appeared in school pageants, but it was not until the family returned to Evanston that he was able to make any serious move towards acting as a career.

Back in Evanston, where he found the busy streets and bustling community a little disturbing after the peace and tranquillity of the forests, he attended Stolp Public Grammar School before moving on to New Trier High School. Reputedly one of the best public schools in America, New Trier is located in neighbouring Winnetka, a suburb of

Chicago. His previous enforced but enjoyable independence gave him some trying moments but he gradually adapted and conformed to the social demands of attending school in an urban community. Small and thin during his early years, he now grew rapidly. He attained his full height of six feet two by the time he was 16, although without putting on much bodily bulk. Despite his reservations about high school, he found a niche in the drama classes and this work, into which he threw himself with wholehearted vigour, led to his winning a scholarship sponsored by the Winnetka Drama Club which took him to Chicago's Northwestern University.

At Northwestern, which had a nationally recognized drama department, he was taught by Alvina Krause. He developed rapidly and was soon playing important roles in dramatic productions. Among the students who passed through Northwestern on their way to Broadway and Hollywood were Patricia Neal, a few years Heston's junior, and Ralph Meeker, a few years his senior. Most important to the aspiring young actor, however, was a young man named David Bradley.

Three years older than Heston, Bradley had been a student at Todd School, Woodstock, Illinois, whose most famous acting alumnus was Orson Welles. Bradley was fascinated by film-making and his early amateur work showed the profound influence Welles had upon him. In 1941 Bradley decided to make a film of *Peer Gynt* and invited Charlton Heston, then aged 17, to play the title role.

Heston accepted readily and as a result found himself involved in a production which was to have a lasting reputation on the art-house circuit.

Peer Gynt was shot silent and in black and white, but the inventive photography of Bradley gave it an elegance and quality which belied its humble origins. As the young and irresponsible globe-trotter who roamed the world from east of the sun to west of the moon, Heston's performance is striking for an actor of his age and inexperience. Years later, he would disarmingly recall that he played the part without any real understanding of the role's nuances or, indeed, that the entire piece had a strong satirical element.

In 1965 a revised version of the film appeared which used the music by Edvard Grieg and had a narration by the distinguished silent movie star Francis X. Bushman, whose career both intersected and mirrored Heston's own. This version of *Peer Gynt* was a marked improvement upon the original, which had used sometimes clumsy title cards, and it gained further plaudits for Bradley.

Heston's life at Northwestern was hectic. His studies and his acting were partly financed by various jobs to help pay his way and he also did some work on local radio in the Chicago area where his already sonorous voice was used to good effect in several dramatic productions.

It was around that time that Chuck, as he was known by almost everyone, met a pretty, dark-haired girl of his own age who was also taking drama classes at Northwestern. She was Lydia Marie Clarke. Clearly their relationship was not exactly love at first sight; indeed, both would later recall that quite the opposite could have been inferred from their argumentative early relationship. As Lydia observed in an interview with Marilyn Funt, she 'thought he was arrogant and conceited, and supremely self-confident.'

Lydia was born in Two Rivers, Wisconsin, where, as a high school senior, she won a national poetry-reading contest; she was therefore not unused to dramatic performance, which perhaps accounted for the readiness with which she changed course after meeting Chuck. In another interview, with the *Sunday People*, she recalled that 'he was a man possessed with acting' and that when they first met 'he turned me away from study as a law student, and made me try to be an actress.'

But by the time of America's entry into World War II they had decided that their frequent arguments really were a sign of something quite the opposite of mutual dislike; and although Lydia resisted the first few proposals of marriage Chuck made, she finally gave in. They were married on 17 March 1944, the eve of Heston's departure on active service. This took him to the Aleutian Islands, that string of dots on the map which stretches bleakly west from Alaska just below the Arctic Circle, where he served as a radio operator in B29s. It was 18 months before the young couple saw one another again. Following his release from the 11th Air Force when the war ended, they took their first steps towards a joint acting career by moving to New York.

They lived in a cold-water flat along 45th Street in the area known as Hell's Kitchen. From this unprepossessing home, with a pickle factory in the basement and an illicit gun-dealer in the room below theirs, Heston visited all the casting offices with little luck but much perseverance. Many years later, during her husband's preparations for his début in London's West End, Lydia would remark to Jonathan Hartman, a struggling young actor who broke all the rules to gain an audition, successfully as it turned out, that Chuck had been obliged to use forceful tactics to bring himself to the attention of casting agencies and producers. During this period both Lydia and Chuck modelled, he for life classes, and the couple just managed to avoid starving. Eventually, their perseverance paid off and they both landed jobs, but not in New York.

Travelling to Asheville, North Carolina, they worked at the Thomas

Wolfe Memorial Theatre. Originally intending to perform just one play, they stayed on and acted in and co-directed several including *State of the Union, Kiss and Tell* and *The Glass Menagerie* before returning to New York. There, Heston won a role in Katharine Cornell's production of *Antony and Cleopatra* at the Martin Beck Theatre. The part, that of Procleius, was small, little more than a step up from the traditional budding actor's role of spear-carrier, but the play had a long run and the experience was invaluable for him. Heston has often remarked that Katharine Cornell was the actress he most admired, and he presumably found working with her pleasurable, although he would later be characteristically dismissive, implying that he won the role only because she was tall and liked to have tall actors around her. The play was directed by Miss Cornell's husband, Guthrie McClintic. Also in the cast were Eli Wallach, not yet a noted exponent of the Method school of acting, and Maureen Stapleton, still three years away from her great Broadway success in *The Rose Tattoo*.

The following year, 1948, the Hestons again moved out of town to work together in summer stock, this time in Pennsylvania. Then it was back to New York for two Broadway plays, neither of which was successful. *Leaf and Bough* was directed by Rouben Mamoulian, whose recent Broadway successes had included *Oklahoma!* and *Carousel*. Heston's notices were better than the play's, which soon closed. In *Cock-a-Doodle-Doo* he worked with Darren McGavin, whose career mixed stage and film work but who has never achieved the success his skills deserve. Heston also appeared in George Bernard Shaw's *The Millionairess* and played Theseus in Racine's *Phaedra*.

Then he received a call from David Bradley and returned to Chicago to play Mark Antony in the young film-maker's production of *Julius Caesar*.

Once again Bradley demonstrated his technical ability, using imaginative camera angles to turn such Chicago landmarks as the Rosenwald Museum into credible Roman buildings. The film as a whole was remarkably impressive, given its tiny budget and the relative inexperience of all the leading players, although Heston was by now gaining rapidly in confidence and ability. His physical appearance was now improved by some additional weight on what had been hitherto a rather awkward and gangling frame. The broken nose which he had acquired during his university footballing forays did nothing to detract from his physical presence. Indeed, these features together with his direct grey-blue eyes, blondish hair and resonant voice, made him a commanding figure.

Adhering closely to Shakespeare's text, Bradley's *Julius Caesar* compares most favourably with other film versions of the play and it is sad that the director never fulfilled his early promise in the world of commercial film-making. Later, Bradley was briefly under contract to MGM, but his commercial career foundered on such rocky projects as *Dragstrip Riot* and *Twelve to the Moon*. He eventually turned to the academic life and in 1975 was professor in film studies at UCLA.

Playing a one-line role in *Julius Caesar* was a young actor named Hank McKinnies, who later changed his name to Jeffrey Hunter and appeared in several films, including *King of Kings* in which he played Jesus Christ. His career was cut tragically short by his death while undergoing surgery following an accident.

When Heston began to acquire a national reputation, *Julius Caesar* was re-released and gained considerable critical acclaim – especially in Europe, where it won an award at the 1953 Locarno Film Festival.

Lydia was also expanding her professional experience by working in Shakespeare, first as an understudy in a Broadway production of *Richard III* but later graduating to a leading role. Her big theatrical break came, however, in a modern play when Sidney Kingsley cast her in his *Detective Story*, a play to which she and her husband would return many times in the future.

The joint successes of the Hestons were rewarded when they were presented with Theatre World Awards as two of the most promising players in America.

These years were, of course, the golden age of American TV drama, and while some stage actors were either unsuited to TV or were unwilling to risk their careers live on camera before millions of viewers, Charlton Heston was eager to face any challenge.

He was successful in obtaining many major roles on TV, several of them in classics, especially in CBS's 'Studio One' series. Once again he played Mark Antony in *Julius Caesar* and he was Rochester in *Jane Eyre*, both for CBS in 1948. The following year he continued attracting attention in *Shadow and Substance*, *Battleship Bismarck*, and as Heathcliff in *Wuthering Heights*. He later appeared as Petruchio in *The Taming of the Shrew* and as Philip Carey in Maugham's *Of Human Bondage*. In 1950 he also undertook his first portrayal of Macbeth, a part he would return to in the theatre time and again over the years. This TV version was directed by Franklin J. Schaffner, who had also directed *Jane Eyre* and with whom Heston would work many times in the future on the big screen.

It was during this stage of Heston's career that he first came to the attention of the film producer and starmaker Hal B. Wallis. First as head of production at Warner Brothers, later as one of Hollywood's leading independent film producers, Wallis was responsible for more than 400 movies, many of which proved to be huge financial successes and simultaneously gained critical acclaim and several Academy Awards. They ranged from *Little Caesar* in 1930 to *Rooster Cogburn* in 1975, along the way including such well-received films as *I Am a Fugitive from a Chain Gang*, *The Life of Emile Zola*, *The Maltese Falcon*, *Casablanca*, *Come Back*, *Little Sheba*, *Becket* and *Barefoot in the Park*. During his career Wallis discovered or gave early breaks to numerous actors who went on to become major international stars.

The exact circumstances of Wallis's discovery of Heston are a little vague. As time passes and memory fades, differing accounts arise about the discoveries of screen actors. In one story Wallis remarks to someone who assures him that a new actor is around who would be the next Burt Lancaster, 'Yes, but do we need another Burt Lancaster?'

Wallis would later assert that he saw all of Heston's CBS TV performances but it seems likely that the producer saw only one, *Jane Eyre*. In the event, it is largely irrelevant. What matters is that Wallis called Heston in and signed him on the spot without even the obligatory screen test with which Wallis had preceded his other signings (which included both Lancaster and Kirk Douglas). Wallis later claimed that the young actor's striking physical presence was the deciding factor and that in any event Heston was wearing a beard at the time (for an unsuccessful Broadway production of *Design for a Stained Glass Window*) so a screen test would not have served much purpose. This somewhat obscure reason for the absence of a screen test may be another example of time changing perspective. Wallis's haste probably owed rather more than he credits to the fact that Warner Brothers were also interested in the young actor and had already offered him their standard contract.

Wallis suggested a better deal. Unlike many contracts, especially the standard studio type, Wallis's allowed considerable freedom and flexibility. True, the contract called for a fixed number of movies, but in between times Heston was free to accept offers for stage and TV work and also to take movie roles offered by other producers. There were also many other beneficial clauses which helped pave the way to Heston soon having more built-in approvals than any young actor could reasonably expect. At the time, perhaps only Marlon Brando had similar benefits. Indeed, the terms of Heston's contract were better than those under which many an established screen actor was obliged to work. Among the approvals he soon had were those of script and casting, areas which would much exercise him in the coming years.

Wallis's offer was snapped up by Heston, who was smart enough to know a good thing when it was dangled before him. What neither Wallis nor Heston can have expected, however, was the staggering amount of publicity all this gave the young actor before he so much as set foot in Hollywood, let alone stood before a camera there.

This publicity stemmed not from the terms of his contract but from the indignation of Warner Brothers when the actor was spirited away from them. The company, and especially Jack Warner, complained loudly and bitterly and the affair reached such proportions that MCA, who were then Heston's agents, were banned from the Warner lot in Hollywood. This meant that all MCA's clients were unrepresented, and as was the practice during such disputes, MCA asked the William Morris agency to step in and hold the fort for their clients while Jack Warner fulminated. Warners said no to this, too, which meant that MCA's clients were without representation, so the Screen Actors' Guild joined the fight in order to protect its members. Such goings-on delighted the press and not only the popular papers took up the story. The tale was featured at length in *The New York Times* in April, 1950 and the paper returned to it again in October of the same year, by which time just about every filmgoer in America was eagerly awaiting the first appearance in a professional movie of this hitherto little-known actor named Charlton Heston.

C H A P T E R
Two

'He looks cheerful . . . a sort of friendly look to him.'
Cecil B. De Mille

During the late 1940s and on into the mid-1950s many American films showed the influences of refugee German directors and photographers who had fled their Nazi-dominated homeland. In Hollywood, they continued to develop the Expressionist cinema which had been much in vogue in Europe through the 1920s and 1930s. Typified by dimly-lit sets, unusual and dramatic camera angles, terse and often enigmatic dialogue, convoluted plots and a harassed and frequently doomed hero, a style of film-making emerged which perfectly suited the hard-boiled school of movies that followed the short-lived gangster genre. With motor-car headlights reflected on rain-slick city streets, fog-bound runways, neon signs half-illuminating dingy hotel bedrooms and harsh shadows cutting across faces that had once been full-lit by the bright studio lights, an intensely dramatic effect was created. For many of the poorer Hollywood studio bosses such techniques had an attraction which had nothing at all to do with aesthetics. Because the settings were so dimly lit they could get away with re-using old sets or cutting corners on new ones. Put simply, these films were cheap to make. But their impact was enormous.

Some years later, the young French critics, led by André Bazin, writing in *Cahiers du Cinéma*, likened this film style to the school of detective fiction exemplified by such writers as Dashiell Hammett, Raymond Chandler, Jim Thompson, James M. Cain and Horace McCoy. The stories of these writers were then appearing in the French pulp magazine *Série Noire* and the term *film noir* was coined to describe the movies which resembled them.

Although failing in some respects to fulfil the inevitably imprecise definition of *film noir*, Heston's first Hollywood movie, *Dark City* (1950), certainly does meet most of the criteria.

Danny Haley (Heston) is a small-time gambler who, in a crooked card game, wins a cheque for a large sum of money from Arthur Winant (Don Defore). This money does not belong to Winant, and in a fit of guilt-induced remorse he kills himself. Unable to cash the cheque because his big-time friends have heard of the loser's death and want to keep their already grubby hands clean of this particular piece of unpleasantness, Danny finds himself between the rock and the hard place when Winant's crazy brother, Sidney (Mike Mazurki), comes after the cardsharps. With two of his comrades murdered by psychotic Sidney, Danny and the fourth gambler, Augie (Jack Webb), set out to find the madman before he finds them. Danny meets his victim's widow, Victoria (Viveca Lindfors), has a brief affair, and is moved by her devotion to her family. Later, after Augie has come to a sticky end, Danny finally meets and defeats Sidney. The experience, and the widow, prove salutory, and he resolves to change his life and settle down with nightclub singer Fran (Lizabeth Scott).

The film's director, William Dieterle, had left Germany in 1930 to begin a long and distinguished career in Hollywood, first with Warner's and later with RKO. *Dark City* is the only *noir*-ish film he made despite his familiarity with the Expressionist style. Among his best-known films are *The Hunchback of Notre-Dame* with Charles Laughton and biopics about Emile Zola and Benito Juarez, both of which were produced by Hal Wallis. Dieterle's cameraman on *Dark City*, Victor Milner, was also a stranger to *film noir*, having built a considerable reputation for his work on several spectacles, including Cecil B. De Mille's 1934 version of *Cleopatra* for which he won an Oscar.

Acting performances in *Dark City* were generally good. Many faces that were to become familiar to film and TV audiences in later years turned up in minor roles, among them that of Ed Begley, an actor of considerable talent who played Broadway, TV and movies with equal skill, and Harry Morgan, who similarly found fame in all areas of acting, especially on TV as Joe Friday's sidekick in *Dragnet* and latterly as Colonel Potter in *M*A*S*H*. As for Joe Friday himself, he was of course played by Jack Webb, whose tersely monosyllabic acting style hardly ever varied. Yet, by some strange alchemy, which he demonstrates here in the role of Augie, he usually contrived to convey characters of resilience and depth.

Women in *film noir* seldom qualify for much more than a swift and sticky end, after being mauled and threatened by villain and hero alike. Here, Viveca Lindfors is good as the widow and Lizabeth Scott does

Watched by nitery chirp Lizabeth Scott, Heston deals a dead man's hand to Don Defore in Dark City.

well enough in her slightly awkward role as what *Variety*'s reviewer termed a 'nitery chirp'.

Until the sudden and somewhat improbable shift in character he is called upon to make in the closing stages of the film, Heston's Danny Haley is cynically persuasive as the small-timer who has few redeeming features and decidedly suspect moral standards. It is this change in character, leading as it does to an upbeat ending of hope for a happy future, that finally deprives the film of true *noir* status. The mood of most of the rest of the film is well within the gloomy ethos, lightened only by frequent chirps from Fran.

Much later Heston would recall *Dark City* as being mediocre, but given the requirements of the day and the fact that the screenplay suffered from too many hands on the typewriter (even if one pair did belong to Ketti Frings who later wrote *Come Back, Little Sheba* and the Pulitzer Prize-winning play *Look Homeward, Angel*), it is not at all a bad début on the national scene. Certainly the role and his performance in it, allied as it was to the pre-production brouhaha in the national press, made moviemakers in Hollywood sit up and take notice, even those as experienced and hard-headed as Cecile B. De Mille.

Then approaching 70, De Mille had not enjoyed a massive success for a number of years although his latest film, *Samson and Delilah*, had enjoyed good box-office despite a mixed critical reaction. Heston had been introduced to De Mille and when he drove past the veteran film-maker one day he smiled and waved. De Mille asked his secretary who it was, and she reminded him; De Mille commented on his friendly smile and then remarked that Heston might be suitable for the role of the circus boss in his new picture. This was *The Greatest Show on Earth* (1952), a film of enormous scope (in which several established stars were scheduled to play roles as circus performers).

Since completing his first Hollywood film and in the absence of any immediate offers, Heston had taken advantage of his flexible contract with Hal Wallis to go back to New York for various TV productions, including the Franklin Schaffner-directed *Macbeth*.

Now, Heston experienced De Mille's habit of describing roles at length to actors without actually offering the part. For several weeks Heston would turn up at the great man's office, listen to his explanations of the role, offer suitable comments when a gap appeared in the monologue, and depart. Eventually, without his having been tested or even having read for it, the part was offered to Heston and snapped up. To play in a Cecil B. De Mille film was bound to be good experience; to play an important part, indeed the pivotal role, was staggering good fortune for the young actor. All the hard years of playing small roles on Broadway and in summer stock, the years of depriving himself and Lydia of normal comforts, were finally paying off.

The storyline of *The Greatest Show on Earth* concerns itself with twin and rather trite love stories and a few sub-plots of even less substance. Elephant girl Angel (Gloria Grahame) and trapeze artist Holly (Betty Hutton) are both in love with ringmaster Brad (Heston), who has no time for anything or anyone outside his first love, which is the circus. After the arrival of Sebastian (Cornel Wilde), who takes the spotlight from Holly with his spectacular trapeze work, the temperature rises outside as well as inside the big top. Meanwhile, Angel's boyfriend Klaus (Lyle Bettger), growing jealous of her attraction to Brad, tries to rob the circus while it is *en route* by rail to its next venue. The robbery comes unstuck and so too does Klaus when his car is hit by the train, which is derailed. Brad strives to save the train but is seriously injured. His life is saved by Buttons the clown (James Stewart), who is really a

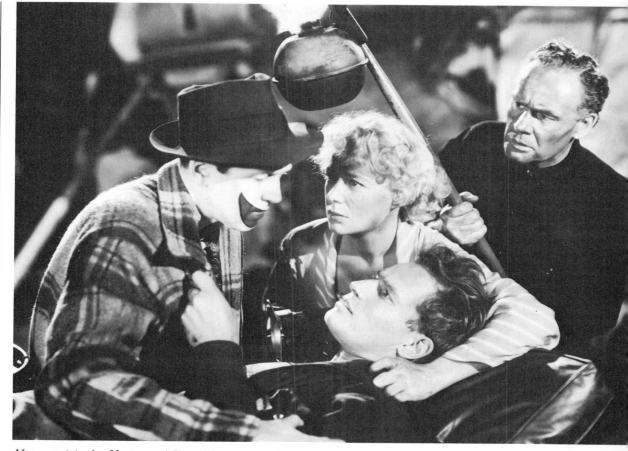

Not surprisingly, Heston and Betty Hutton are unhappy at the bedside manner of doctor-in-disguise James Stewart in The Greatest Show on Earth.

doctor on the run for murder. All ends happily with Sebastian taking up with Angel, thus leaving Brad to realize the error of his single-minded ways and take Holly in his arms.

Being a picture about the circus, and a De Mille picture into the bargain, none of the banalities of the storyline matters very much, for the true star of the movie is the circus itself (actually Ringling Brothers) and while the acts are 'on' the film never flags (except, perhaps, for those who do not like circuses).

Cornel Wilde, who had the musculature to carry the role of a trapeze artist, does well enough but lacks the spark needed to lift him as far above the sawdust as his role demands. Although a serious and dedicated film-maker, Wilde never quite made it to the big time even though, as lately as December 1985, having just remarried at the age of 70, he was still hoping to return to the screen in a role worthy of his long-buried talents.

As the other trapeze artist, Betty Hutton brings considerable vivacity to the movie, just as she had to a number of screen musicals, most notably as Annie Oakley in *Annie Get Your Gun*. Hers is just one of many sad tales from Hollywood. After completing work on *The Greatest Show on Earth* she made one more movie that same year, then walked out on her contract because the studio would not let her husband direct her in films. Five years later she made one more film, then drifted into comparative obscurity before quitting in the middle of making another film in 1962. When she filed for bankruptcy it was revealed that she had somehow gone through about $10 million. She then spent many years as a voluntary psychiatric patient, after which she lived a quiet life in Connecticut.

In the pivotal role of the circus ringmaster, Heston's performance is accomplished and he maintains a dignified central presence amidst the shenanigans all around him. Indeed, his mild aloofness caused one lady to compliment De Mille on the manner in which he had managed to make the circus's real-life ringmaster fit in so well with all those professional movie actors.

The film itself won the Oscar for Best Picture, made more money than Angel's elephants could carry and, most important of all for Heston, made producers sit up and take notice of this new actor in their midst.

His next film did not, however, capitalize upon the good start he had made in Hollywood. In the early 1950s the motion-picture industry was going through one of its occasional sackcloth-and-ashes periods. On the receiving end of the forced humility this time was the Native American, or, as he had hitherto been called, the Red Indian. Unfortunately, any attempts at rehabilitation of the race that had been systematically abused and patronized by film-makers for half a century (after a couple of centuries of equally systematic but real genocide) were rather badly undercut by the decision to cast white men and women in the leading Indian roles. Burt Lancaster played an Indian, as did Jeff Chandler. Donna Reed had a fling (in a later Heston movie), Debra Paget built a career out of playing Indian maidens and even such unlikely ladies as Audrey Hepburn and Jennifer Jones were squeezed in by playing girls of mixed race. This failure to pit principles against probable audience resistance makes it difficult to avoid responding with cynicism to the movies which resulted.

Hollywood quickly discovered that one of the easiest ways out of its self-imposed dilemma of being unwilling to use real Indian actors was to concoct a tale about white children captured by savages, brought up by them, and then faced with choosing between their real and their adopted brethren. It was this latter, hackneyed course that was adopted for *The Savage* (1952), in which Charlton Heston plays a white man who has grown up among the Sioux.

Given the essentially patronizing tone of the format the film was not too bad and the Indians emerge from it with a measure of dignity despite having to mouth dialogue that no one outside a motion-picture studio would ever hear spoken by anyone of any race.

Warily watching the white man's world from behind his Sioux warpaint in The Savage.

The story calls for Warbonnet (Heston), who is really Jim Aherne, to return to the white man's world and intercede between soldiers and Indians in a doomed attempt to bring peace to both his peoples. In its way Warbonnet/Aherne was a very poor forerunner to the kind of role which the actor would encounter many times in later years: the man of principle who is prepared to sacrifice all, even his life, for the greater well-being of his fellow men, usually an oppressed race. That it doesn't work here is a failing of the screenplay, not the performer.

Warbonnet, raised by the Sioux after his family has been murdered by a band of Crow Indians (a tribe against which Hollywood screenwriters appear to have the longest-lasting feud in the history of interracial conflict), is sent to the nearest army command post to spy on the white man's activities. In so doing he will also set at rest the minds of those Indians who do not trust him. Among those who *do* feel he is to be trusted is Luta (Joan Taylor), but he is unaware of her love for him. Later when Warbonnet, now in the guise of Jim Aherne, scout, leads a group of soldiers into Indian territory he abruptly abandons them when he learns that Luta has been kidnapped by Crows. After freeing her, Warbonnet is fired upon by the same soliders and Luta is killed. Now totally committed to fighting the white man, Warbonnet helps prepare an ambush but at the last moment cannot let the trap be sprung. Part of the internal conflict with which he is wrestling is the fact that he has met Tally Hathersall (Susan Morrow), with whom he is falling in love. He warns the soldiers and the women and children they are accompanying. According to Indian tradition (or, at least, to Hollywood-Indian tradition), Warbonnet's adoptive father has to kill him. The old man goes through the motions but the wound is not fatal.

Warbonnet, who now resumes his real identity as Jim Aherne, returns to the white side of the fence and a life with the girl he loves, a union which neatly symbolizes peace between white man and Indian.

Given the essentially trite nature of the plot and the elementary screenplay, which allows for nothing other than routine stereotyping, *The Savage* barely makes the grade, even as a B-western. Yet it is of interest because in its hero it foreshadows the kind of role Heston would encounter so often in the future. Here, obviously unaware of what Hollywood's would-be image-makers had in store for him, he does reasonably well within the part's limitations. Had he known what the future held he might well have tried harder – or, maybe, tried not at all.

An essential problem here is the lack of humanity the Warbonnet/Aherne character is allowed to display. Perhaps an actor with a longer string of movies behind him might have called for changes which would allow him to impart some hint of the complex nature which lies inside all men. True, some excuse can be found in Hollywood's traditional view of the native-American, which bears a remarkable resemblance to a cigar-store Indian. Unfortunately, Hollywood had long since decreed that Indians were expressionless stoics and Heston, doubtless finding kinship in this restraint of emotion, however false in its premise, settled for conformity.

Next came a much better effort all round: none the less, *Ruby Gentry* (1952) has received surprisingly poor critical response.

Set in a Southern town worthy of Tennessee Williams at his steamiest, the story tells of Ruby Gentry (Jennifer Jones) and her paranoid determination to destroy everyone who ever snubbed her during her rise from poor-girl-from-the-wrong-side-of-the-tracks to wife of the community's richest man. Although in love with Boake Tackman (Heston), the scion of the now-poor aristocrats who once ruled this part of the world, she sees him marry another woman for her money in order that he can reclaim the local swamplands and restore his family's fortunes. On the rebound from Boake, Ruby marries recently widowed Jim Gentry (Karl Malden). When he dies, she discovers that not only do the local people all think she is responsible for her husband's death but that most of them also owe him money. She decides to take her revenge by ruining every last one of them.

She destroys the work Boake has done, reflooding his lands, and he in turn takes his revenge upon her, an attack which ends in a sexual assault. This physical contact, violent though it is, re-sparks their love, but before she can do anything to restore their relationship, her crazy brother, Jewel (James Anderson), kills Boake. Ruby then kills her brother and all ends in a bloody welter of grim despair with the survivors being just about as unhappy as it is possible to be.

The film is often slow-moving but it has many splendid moments, mostly achieved through the skill of director King Vidor, whose career had begun in 1919 and included many highly successful films including *The Big Parade* (1925), *The Crowd* (1928), *Hallelujah* (1928) and *The Fountainhead* (1949).

Vidor had directed Jennifer Jones in *Duel in the Sun* (1947), and although harassed by her husband, producer David O. Selznick, who streamed countless numbers of his infamous memos at any film-maker who came anywhere near his wife, he drew an intensely dramatic performance from an actress who usually appeared to be working under stress, possibly a side-effect of her awareness of all those memos. Alert to the interference potential of Selznick, Vidor insisted that his contract for *Ruby Gentry* should include a clause which kept his star's husband off the set. This did not prevent the familiar barrage of memos but Vidor ignored them, having discovered over the years that Selznick's instructions had a habit of cancelling themselves out. At one point, when Selznick threatened to pull his wife off the movie, Vidor weakened, but for the most part the only serious effect Selznick had was on the clothes the costume department provided for Jennifer Jones.

The role of Ruby certainly had more depth than many Miss Jones tackled. As Vidor later observed, Ruby bore 'deep scars, she's marked by [her] environment, also by the fact that she nourishes a fierce hatred in her breast. She cannot forgive, but she can go on fighting.' She certainly could. In one scene, when called upon to slap her co-star's face, Miss Jones complied with such vigour that she broke a bone in her hand.

The scene in which Ruby Gentry and Boake Tackman hunt one another through the swamp is a notably erotic piece of film-making, given the time and circumstances of its filming. Perhaps the inherent sexism of a screenplay which makes the victim of a near-rape fall in love with her attacker does not sit too well with today's audience but, this caveat aside, the film stands up better today than many of its contemporary melodramas.

This swamp scene is well-lit and photographed (by Russell Harlan, who became Howard Hawks' favourite cameraman) and belies its location in a Hollywood studio tank.

The supporting performances of James Anderson and Karl Malden are both good. Malden had just won the Oscar as Best Supporting Actor for his role in *A Streetcar Named Desire*.

Heston's performance is solid and workmanlike, but in the scenes with Miss Jones he opens up far more than he had in his previous films, and indeed more than he would in most of his later roles, in which his response towards his female co-stars appears to have been conditioned by a growing disenchantment with screen actresses.

Next came another western, this time a mildly tongue-in-cheek foray into the never-was of America's past. In *Pony Express* (1953) Buffalo Bill Cody (Heston) and Wild Bill Hickok (Forrest Tucker) vie with one another for girls, money and lasting fame, and provided no one takes the ensuing scraps and derring-do too seriously the romp is fairly enjoyable.

Buffalo Bill meets Evelyn Hastings (Rhonda Fleming, always too stately and glamorous for westerns) and her brother Rance (Michael Moore) while he is helping extend the Pony Express line to California, thus linking the west coast with the Union. They are not pleased by the impending link, for they have plans to turn California into an independent republic, a well-meant scheme in which they are being

Helping Forrest Tucker defend the honour of Rhonda Fleming and Jan Sterling in Pony Express.

manipulated by Cooper (Henry Brandon), a rascally stageline operator, and Pemberton (Stuart Randall), an agent for a foreign power
which has designs on California. Also involved is Denny Russell (Jan
Sterling), a young lady of doubtful morals who goes the way of all such
ladies in this grade of western and dies in defence of the hero, thus
leaving him free to frolic with someone of unimpeachable, if not
positively unimpregnable, virtue.

Almost everything in the film is highly forgettable, but the playing of
Heston and Tucker is always lively and pleasurable. The action
sequences are very much in accordance with the requirements of the
front-row cowboys at whom this type of movie was aimed and whose
critical standards most moviemakers seem to have held in pretty low
regard.

It is unfortunate that the admittedly light-hearted approach of the film was not allowed much freer rein. Had *Pony Express* been made as an out-and-out comedy it would have been a better film and, more important to Heston, it would have allowed him an opportunity to apply his greatly under-used ability to play lightweight roles. But this may well have been too early for film-makers to risk joking with a real-life (if larger-than-life), all-American hero. Many years on Paul Newman would do just that with the same Buffalo Bill Cody, mildly uneasy in the task though he may have been. It was also too early for Heston to tinker with popular historical figures. Even later in his career he has displayed a high regard for such men, even when, as in the case of Cody, they have not always justified deference. In the event, caught between pulp-fiction heroics and factual narrative, he brings to the part much more weight than it can really withstand.

The director of *Pony Express* was Jerry Hopper, who would crop up behind the camera for several Heston movies and also one in which Lydia made her bid for Hollywood stardom.

For his next film, Heston was required to age gradually from being young to being very old, the first of many such roles that he would play. This was also the first of two films in which he played the part of a man he held in high esteem. President Andrew Jackson, Heston has remarked, is 'in my list of the greatest five or six people America has ever produced. [He is] a greatly underrated man.'

The President's Lady (1953) takes the story of Old Hickory from his early years until the eve of his election as President of the United States.

In this version of his life, the film's makers concentrate upon the love story between Jackson (Heston) and Rachel Robards (Susan Hayward). When they first meet she is married, but she soon divorces her husband Lewis (Whitfield Connor) and marries Jackson. Unfortunately, the divorce has not been finalized, but this fact is not discovered until some years later. By this time Jackson has become very well known and he and Rachel are subjected to much abuse. The divorce is finally settled and the couple once again go through the marriage ceremony. This is not enough for some people, however, and at a party Charles Dickinson (Carl Betz) remarks that Jackson has stolen another man's wife. Incensed, Jackson challenges him to a duel, kills Dickinson and is himself wounded. Despite this he assures Rachel that he will compensate her for all these slights by raising her above any further insults.

Jackson hits the campaign trail but Rachel's health is failing and, at a rally, as he speaks to a crowd of voters, she faints when a heckler remarks that 'no one wants a woman of ill-repute as a first lady'.

Jackson goes on to win the election, thus completing the log-cabin-to-White-House cycle so beloved of many Americans, not least those in charge of the nation's on-screen image, but Rachel dies before his inauguration.

Measured in financial terms, *The President's Lady* was not a successful picture, but despite being necessarily static it contains fine performances and benefits from a literate, if rather wordy, script. Both the principals perform very well indeed, striking a comfortable note in their on-screen relationship. As observed earlier, with the passage of time Heston's attitude towards his female co-stars was gradually to harden into general disapproval if not downright animosity. Just as his pairing with Jennifer Jones brought an unusual emotional intensity, so this coupling with Susan Hayward drew from him a rare display of natural ease.

His scenes with Miss Hayward apart, Heston brings to the role of Old Hickory a commendable dignity which is in keeping with the high regard in which he holds the real man. Given the rough and ready nature of early American politics (which has not softened all that much over the years), it may well be that Heston's view of Jackson makes him out to be slightly more statesmanlike than was really the case. Nevertheless, there is a quality of command in his portrayal which well fits the probable reality of the man. This is conveyed by Heston in a manner which is just as natural as in the playing of his scenes with Susan Hayward.

The next few years were bad ones for Susan Hayward. In 1955 she attempted suicide and the same year worked on *The Conqueror*, the ill-fated movie of whose cast (including Miss Hayward and John Wayne) and technicians an abnormally high percentage developed illnesses apparently attributable to working on location in the American deserts during atomic bomb tests.

For Charlton Heston, it was back to the wild and woolly West for his next film – and this marked a downturn of this switchback period in his career. *Arrowhead* (1953) was another highly forgettable movie. In it, Heston portrays Indian scout Ed Bannon, who is loosely based upon the real-life character Al Sieber (whose escapades have provided the jumping-off point for half-a-dozen Hollywood westerns).

Bannon is constantly at odds with the army for whom he works, but he is the only man around who believes the Indians, led by the villainous Toriano (Jack Palance), will resist being moved to a reservation. As he suspects, Toriano leads a revolt. Although some films of the mid-1950s were taking the Indians' side, in this instance such lack of co-operation in their own destruction is taken as being bad for American society. Bannon has to put things right, and if the army can't do it he will. Instead of killing the Indians wholesale (as he was wont to do earlier in the film), he opts instead for the hand-to-hand combat so beloved of Hollywood screenwriters. As usual the white man wins, the bad Indian is killed and all the others prove their inherent goodness by allowing themselves to be led off meekly to despair and slow death of spirit and body in the Florida Everglades. *Arrowhead* is not a good picture and no one emerges from it with very much credit, which is unfortunate given the talent on hand.

The director, who also wrote the screenplay based upon the novel by W. R. Burnett, was Charles Marquis Warren, whose dedication to the myth of the Old West helped him create several of the most popular TV westerns, among them *Gunsmoke*, *The Virginian* and *Rawhide*, the series which launched Clint Eastwood on his career.

Jack Palance has always been a much better actor than Hollywood has allowed him to be. Following serious burns inflicted while flying bombers during World War II, he underwent plastic surgery which helped give him a decidedly unHollywood look. For a while he was given roles as untrustworthy Indians or Mexicans (frequently inter-changeable no-goods in the movies), despite having gained a considerable reputation for his work in TV, especially for his superb performance in the lead in *Requiem for a Heavyweight*.

For Heston, the part of Ed Bannon had more texture than most leading roles in westerns of comparable grade and era, but this was still only trivial stuff. While his performance is far from perfunctory there is too much for him to grit his teeth over and not enough to sink them into.

Things didn't improve very much with *Bad for Each Other* (1953), which tells the well-used tale of an idealistic doctor, Tom Owen (Heston), who allows himself to be diverted towards wealthy patients only to be saved from his baser instincts by a local disaster. Although based upon a short story by the usually excellent Horace McCoy, who also co-scripted the film, this particular kind of tale was told to much better effect in A. J. Cronin's *The Citadel*. Somewhat uncomfortable as the dedicated medic (although nowhere nearly as miscast as Robert Mitchum was to be as another medic in *Not as a Stranger* a couple of years later), Heston did what he could, but never seems to be at ease in a city suit, least of all one worn by a doctor. The outer trappings of his roles had even now begun to exert a peculiar hold on Heston and to bring to bear some degree of restraint upon his ability to immerse himself in a character. Unlike, say, Marlon Brando, his close contemporary, Heston approached his parts from the outside, a method he continued to employ as his career blossomed. Brando, a year younger than Heston, in keeping with his non-traditional stage training, went inside – albeit occasionally so far inside as to become a shade indistinguishable. Of the screen roles Brando had played up to this point in time, only one, that of Emiliano Zapata, had called for heavy make-up, and while Brando's 1953 role as Mark Antony was one which Heston had already played as a very young man, and would later return to, it is hard to imagine Heston tackling, let alone mastering, the Brando role in *The Men* or that of Stanley Kowalski in *A Streetcar Named Desire* – even less the black-clad bike-rider in *The Wild One*. The American stage, which had bred both men, had certainly proved itself to be far from uniform in the nature and style of the actors it produced.

Quite clearly, *Bad for Each Other* did little to further Heston's career and is fortunately seldom seen today. Even the presence of German-born Franz Planer behind the camera could not save it. Planer, who coincidentally also photographed the Mitchum movie, would later work with Heston to much better effect. A further coincidence is that Planer shot *The Caine Mutiny*, the stage version of which Heston would bring to London more than 30 years later. Lydia Heston played a small role in *Bad for Each Other*.

The Naked Jungle (1953) gave Heston an opportunity to play a character with few saving graces, the first such role since his Hollywood début as Danny Haley.

Attempting to patch up an uneasy relationship with Eleanor Parker in The Naked Jungle.

Based upon Carl Stephenson's short story *Leiningen Versus the Ants*, the story concerns Christopher Leiningen (Heston), who owns a massive plantation in South America which he carved out of swampland and jungle many years ago. Now, wanting to share his land and fine home with someone, he marries by proxy, but when Joanna (Eleanor Parker) arrives he discovers that she has been married before, and he cannot accept this. Their uneasy relationship deteriorates rapidly and she decides to pack her bags and return home. Before she can do so, however, he learns that a massive army of soldier ants is heading their way, and when all his native workers wisely head for the hills Joanna stays on to help defend their home. As the massed ranks of ants draw closer, wiping out everything in their path, Leiningen begins blowing up bridges and pathways, all to no avail. Eventually, he realizes that the only way to stop the ants is to blow the dam holding back the water — which will make his land a swamp again. He successfully destroys the dam and the water floods in, but the house withstands the pressure and Leiningen and his wife survive to start all over again.

Heston's performance in this role, shifting from an emotionless near-tyrant to a more vulnerable but still hard-shelled man by the end, is thoughtfully realized. Eleanor Parker also plays well, countering her co-star's grim attitude towards life and the environment with intelligent good humour.

Although apparently fortuitous, the screenplay of *The Naked Jungle* makes a case for more attention being paid to tailoring roles to suit the traits of the performers cast in them. Admittedly, most actors would prefer to adjust, chameleon-like, but some, of whom Heston is an obvious example, have built up many defence mechanisms. In Heston's case this is so pronounced that his ability to shade a part is sometimes affected. Here, playing a man whose shell is part and parcel of his character, Heston is more at ease than would be those actors who prefer to display open vulnerability.

The special effects, which are most impressive, were devised by producer George Pal, who was responsible for some of the best science-fiction films of the era (among them *Destination Moon*, *When Worlds Collide* and *War of the Worlds*, for which he won three of his five Oscars). The closing scenes of the film, when the ants arrive at the plantation and are destroyed, do not dissipate the suspense that has been created up to that point while the human actors await what has been, until now, an invisible enemy.

Having survived South American ants, albeit from the comparative safety of a Hollywood studio, Heston moved on to another role in a movie with a South American setting. *Secret of the Incas* (1954) is the story of a pair of amoral adventurers, Harry Steele (Heston) and Ed Morgan (Thomas Mitchell), who are seeking a priceless Inca jewel. They are accompanied on their quest by a true archaeologist, Dr Stanley Moorehead (Robert Young), and various other interested parties including Elena Antonescu (Nicole Maurey, whose presence appears to be primarily to provide the required but unintegrated love interest and a possible distribution deal for the film in Europe). In one guise or another, this tale had been told a score of times before by Hollywood, often to prop up some of the weaker Tarzan movies; but this particular version is not too bad. Indeed, some of the scenery, shot in Peru at Macchu Picchu, is superb. The performances are, in the main, perfunctory, with Heston starting out much as he began in the role of Christopher Leiningen but never softening. This absence of shading was a failing which began to appear in some of his less well-developed roles. The much-valued script approval failed to come to his aid here, but it did not matter too much as the film was essentially a straightforward adventure yarn.

The director was again Jerry Hopper and the film also boasts an appearance by a currently popular recording artist (always a sure sign that someone at Head Office has doubts about the product). This time the singer was Yma Sumac, who possessed a voice with a startling range and whose publicity declared she was born on a Peruvian mountain top. Her decriers claimed she was born in Brooklyn but had had the wit to capitalize on her genuinely unusual vocal characteristics by turning her name around from plain Amy Camus.

Although extremely busy making movies in the early 1950s, Heston managed to find time for other ventures too. He returned to the stage, playing Macbeth in Bermuda in 1954; and in the same year he was down at Palm Beach with *Mr Roberts*. Later in the decade he again appeared in *Mr Roberts*, this time at Newport, Rhode Island and at New York's City Center where the director was John Forsythe (who became well-known to TV audiences the following year for the long-running series *Bachelor Father* and even better-known a quarter-century later when he appeared as Blake Carrington in *Dynasty*).

Brooks Atkinson, reviewing *Mr Roberts* in *The New York Times*, wrote that 'Charlton Heston, rangy and deliberate, plays Mister Roberts with relish, amiability and intelligence.'

Heston, co-starring with his wife, toured extensively in *Detective Story*, the Sidney Kingsley play which had been an important milestone in Lydia's early stage career.

Lydia's career had also expanded into the movies. She played the lead in *The Atomic City* (1952), in which her co-star was Gene Barry. Also in the film was that fine character actor Milburn Stone, who appeared in two of her husband's westerns, *The Savage* and *Arrowhead*. Lydia's director was Jerry Hopper, somewhat happier in the New Mexico desert than he had been in his films with her husband.

The Atomic City is a suspense thriller telling the story of the kidnap of an atomic scientist's son, and, while it is routine, it did have the benefit of above-average performances and script. The studio, Paramount, was ecstatic about its leading lady, announcing that as a 'result of her sensitive portrayal of the wife of a young nuclear physicist, film critics are predicting that it will be only a matter of months before Lydia joins the list of established Hollywood stars'. Not for the first time, a studio guessed wrong, but here the reason was less commonplace. Instead of abandoning stardom for high-jinks, or failing to attain it through lack of real talent, this particular actress was about to choose home life instead of a professional career.

Just as Lydia had begun making a practice of travelling with her husband to locations for his work, he went down to New Mexico with her for the filming near Los Alamos. But both Chuck and Lydia had ambitions for a settled domestic life, not the easiest of goals for a movie star to achieve. To this end he had used some of the first money he earned in Hollywood to purchase 1400 acres of woodland around Russell Lake in Michigan, close to his boyhood home of St Helen. They also began building a home on a ridge in Coldwater Canyon, Hollywood. But most important of all was the birth of a son, on 12 February 1955. He was christened Fraser Clarke, a name that preserved both Lydia's family name, Clarke, and a Scottish link which extended through both of Heston's parents, his mother being descended from members of the Fraser clan.

From this point on, Lydia was less often able to accompany her husband on his location trips. This caused some problems, though not those usually associated with movie stars on the loose in foreign parts. In the Hestons' case such separations were not a signal for abandoning all marital restraints but caused instead a measure of depression. Of the two of them it was he who could more readily overcome the problem through immersion in his work.

There was still TV work to be had, and Heston made *Forbidden Area* in CBS's 'Playhouse 90' series; but he bowed out of *Requiem for a Heavyweight*, which perhaps turned out for the best as Jack Palance's portrayal proved to be one of the many highlights of this superb series. Later in the decade Heston made *Point of No Return* for 'Playhouse 90' and he also worked on CBS's 'Medallion Theatre' and 'Climax' series and played in *Along Came Jones* for NBC.

Despite all these professional and personal activities, Heston was also finding more and more time for something which was steadily becoming a near-obsession. Given the nature of the obsessions which afflict many people both inside and outside showbusiness, tennis is probably one of the least injurious. Indeed, as he now needed continual exercise to keep in shape, tennis proved useful. As the years passed, Heston's ability reached a high standard and he played regularly with some of the world's best tennis stars, never seeming to mind that in this pursuit, at least, he usually took second billing.

The films Heston was continuing to make were still a mixed bag, with none really taking advantage of either his capacity for major roles, which he regularly demonstrated on stage or TV, or of his commanding physical presence.

He was on the adventure trail again in *The Far Horizons* (1955), another one of Hollywood's regular trips into the real past in search of something it could bowdlerize.

Based upon the true tale of explorers Merriwether Lewis (Fred MacMurray) and William Clark (Heston), the film follows the two men as they chart the lands President Thomas Jefferson acquired from Napoleon in 1803. The Louisiana Purchase brought to America a vast tract of land stretching from the Gulf of Mexico almost to the Canadian border and from the Mississippi to beyond the Rocky Mountains.

Although the real-life tales of those hardy white men who first travelled the American West are packed with enthralling and exciting adventures, Hollywood managed to make a dog's breakfast of most of its attempts to portray them on-screen. In later years Heston would be involved with one of the better efforts in a story of the larger-than-life mountain men but this time, dealing with the relatively staid explorers Lewis and Clark, the quality of the product was abysmal.

Other real-life characters in the film include the French-Canadian explorer Charbonneau (·Alan Reed) and his Indian companion Saca-jawea (Donna Reed), who is here reduced from her real-life status of a brave and determined guide to providing the mid-script love interest.

Afflicted with a screenplay which included some unbelievably bad dialogue (witness an exchange between explorers and President: 'Oh, congratulations on the Louisiana Purchase') and lacklustre direction by Rudolph Maté, the actors stumble on as best they can.

Some of the stiffness of the two leads may be excused on the grounds that the real-life explorers could well have been ill-at-ease in the

palatial city dwellings of their fellow Americans, but in reality it is evident that Heston and MacMurray were very different types of performer who must have found difficulty in blending. MacMurray was always best at portraying modern, urban men, and highly sophisticated ones at that. Sometimes he played fluffy parts, and even when given a powerful and demanding role such as that of Walter Neff in *Double Indemnity* he brought to it undercurrents of wry humour. Here, as a hardened explorer, he is clearly out of place. Whether intended or not, the impression is gained that Heston made an attempt to adapt to MacMurray's light style. If so, it does not quite work – a certain awkwardness of manner is noticeable; it is fortunate, however, that MacMurray did not attempt to bend to Heston's more dignified style, which would have been even less likely to succeed.

Ultimately, the fate of *Far Horizons* is that it simply does not work. Judging by movies like this, which tell of early American adventure and exploration, it is difficult to believe that those early pioneers ever got off the beach, let alone made it far enough west to build Hollywood.

Heston's next film, *The Private War of Major Benson* (1955), was genuinely intended as a comedy.

After getting on the wrong side of the army through his hard-nosed attitude towards his men, Major Benson (Heston) is sent off to a boys' school to act as training officer for the cadet corps. The discovery that his new charges range in age from six to sixteen, and that the school is run by nuns, causes the major to take to the bottle. Eventually buckling down to it, he employs his usual methods with the boys and succeeds only in alienating them. Married to the army, he also makes a mess of trying to date the school's pretty doctor, Kay Lambert (Julie Adams). His storm-the-barricades tactics are not helped by his inability to shake off the school's tiniest soldier, Cadet Tiger Flaherty (Tim Hovey), who follows him everywhere. In time, Benson softens towards, or rather is softened by, his charges, and although they have been trying to have him recalled to the army they eventually back him wholeheartedly and become a crack squad of cadets. Restored to the good graces of his commanding officer, General Ramsey (Milburn Stone), Benson is given a new, adult, command and also finally succeeds in winning the doctor's affections.

Although the role was seemingly intended for Cary Grant, the part of Major Benson appears tailor-made for Heston, allowing him as it does quietly to send up his screen persona as a no-nonsense tough guy. He

Ill-at-ease with script, director and one another, Heston and Fred MacMurray at last see eye-to-eye in The Far Horizons.

even survives the experience of appearing with a screenful of children, even one with as much and as calculated a scene-stealing potential as young Tiger. With good support from such distinguished character actors as Milburn Stone and the splendid William Demarest in the role of the school caretaker (Demarest was also in *The Far Horizons*), Heston carries the film. It is also well directed, by Jerry Hopper – who also appeared to have found his niche. By his performance Heston proved to anyone who cared to take the hint that he was more than capable of playing comedy.

No one appeared to notice, however, and he was soon up to his neck in soapsuds for *Lucy Gallant* (1955). Once more this was a tale which had been filmed before (and has been done again since). Lucy (Jane Wyman) is left standing at the altar and instead of marriage settles for opening up the biggest dress shop in Texas. Her dedication to selling frocks by the carload blinds her to the fact that rich rancher Casey Cole (Heston) is in love with her, but eventually, after he has made his point (somewhat obscurely) by joining the army and becoming a hero, she jettisons the rag-trade and joins him. It is all pretty mindless nonsense, albeit backed up by good performances from the cast. This also included Claire Trevor (playing a character known as Lady Macbeth), wisecracking Thelma Ritter and, again, William Demarest. Demarest's film career began just as the talkies were coming in; he appeared with Al Jolson in *The Jazz Singer* in 1927 and then matched that 20 years on by appearing in *The Jolson Story*, for which role he was nominated for an Oscar.

Lucy Gallant shows Heston entirely miscast in a part which needed only slight adjustment to make it a Rock Hudson role. Indeed, a year earlier Hudson had played Bob Merrick in *Magnificent Obsession*, which this film superficially resembles. In that opus, the character and the actor, especially the actor, would have dumped little Lucy into a heap of her own lacy lingerie and departed, never to return. That Heston does not blend into his soft surroundings here is partially a mark against him as an actor but much more a criticism of the inanity of film-makers who persistently fail to observe the distinction between casting actors who have clout with the public and those who can actually be expected to play the part well.

In many ways this misuse of Heston's talents since his early impact in *The Greatest Show on Earth* was typical of Hollywood, and an actor with less determination to succeed might well have allowed himself to be buried by the weight of ten or more indifferent movies. Fortunately, Heston was as tough as his on-screen image, and he managed to weather these patchy years. Just as importantly, he was learning his

Quietly sending up his tough-guy image in The Private War of Major Benson *with Tim Hovey and Julie Adams.*

trade and proving himself to be at all times prepared and reliable. Writing of these early years in his autobiography, Hal Wallis, who had done so much to set Heston's film career under way, remarked, 'He was, and always will be, a true professional.'

What he needed now were good roles in first-rate productions. He can scarcely have expected, however, that among the film-makers hovering in the wings and about to make a substantial mark on his career were two such widely contrasting giants of the screen as Orson Welles and, once again, Cecil B. De Mille.

CHAPTER
Three

'If you can't make a career out of two De Mille
pictures, you'll never do it.'
Charlton Heston

Cecil B. De Mille had first made *The Ten Commandments* as a silent
movie in 1923 when he was in his early forties. He returned to it in his
mid-seventies, doubtless aware that in the new age of multi-million-
dollar financing and the long-term undertakings that epics demanded,
this was to be his last major production.

The Bible had proved extraordinarily fruitful for De Mille, and if his
use of the stories of the Old Testament was sometimes a mite gaudy, he
overcame such deficiencies through his ability to pace his movies. Even
the most elaborate tales, decked as they were in sets of staggering
complexity (and cost) and peopled with casts that really were numbered in thousands, were usually whisked along with commendable
speed amidst all the splendour. It was just as well that this was so,
because the scripts were often peppered with Hollywood-isms that
suggest the writers had never so much as seen a Bible, let alone opened
one. The leading actors were also up against problems in De Mille's
movies. It was very easy to get lost in the mass of visual detail with
which the veteran film-maker flooded the screen.

For his original version, De Mille had taken his crew on location to
Guadalupe, a small town on the beach 200 miles north of Los Angeles.
When he was through, the latterday Hollywood-Egyptian artefacts
were left where they lay, with De Mille observing that they might well
set an archaeological problem for future generations. In the event, 1985
saw a pair of eager film buffs raising the money for what must surely be
the strangest 'dig' of all time.

There was never any doubt that Heston would play the role of Moses in De Mille's The
Ten Commandments.

When it came to remaking the film, however, De Mille wanted something rather more impressive than Californian sand dunes. This time he wanted the real thing, which meant on-location filming in Egypt. It took time for him to convince the studio bosses that they should finance a movie which would clearly cost a great deal of money and take a long time to shoot. When they finally gave him the green light they can hardly have expected it would cost what was to be a record sum for the time, in excess of $13 million, or that shooting alone would last about nine months (in all the film was almost two years in the making).

For the role of Moses the Lawgiver, De Mille appears never to have been in any doubt that he wanted Charlton Heston. Apart from liking Heston as an individual, De Mille was impressed by his professionalism and by the remarkable resemblance between a bearded Heston and the Michelangelo image of Moses. Neither can it have escaped the old film-maker's notice that Heston's public image of uprightness and clean living, which he so much admired, was a true reflection of his real-life behaviour. De Mille was shrewd enough to know that he could not risk the role to anyone whose private life was the least sullied.

For Heston, the role was as much a gift from God as the Tablets were to Moses. With this role he could hardly help but become an international star of the first magnitude. Nevertheless, he was neither foolish enough, nor so blasé, as to imagine that he could sit back and coast through the movie.

He threw himself into the part with a degree of enthusiasm that must have been highly gratifying for De Mille. Already noted for the care with which he prepared for his roles, especially any which called upon a measure of historical verisimilitude, Heston studied the Old Testament and the work of biblical scholars. He became thoroughly immersed in the part, even to the point of remaining aloof from fellow actors and extras. The latter, drawn from the location where they were filming in Egypt, regarded Heston with awe and he responded by determining never to behave like a movie actor when he was in their presence. He did not even allow himself the relaxation of lounging about drinking coffee between takes. His habit of walking off into the desert for solitary contemplation before a take also aided this air of controlled detachment, which undoubtedly added a resonance to the interplay between Moses and his people when the cameras eventually turned. The role also had its effect upon the actor himself. When asked during a 1958 interview on British television whether playing Moses had been a religious experience, he refused to be drawn on his private views but remarked, 'I will go so far as to say I did my first shot in that film

Banished from the Pharaoh's court, Heston is soon up to his knees among the brickmakers . . .

. . . a much less privileged place than the one he occupied between Cedric Hardwicke (Sethi) and Yul Brynner (Rameses).

walking barefoot down Mount Sinai, and you don't feel quite the same having done that as before you did it.'

For the most part, the screenplay takes its storyline from the Bible, without too many of the often grotesque infelicities Hollywood brought to other tales from the same source. Nevertheless, the 30-year gap in the Bible's account of Moses' life, between childhood and manhood, allowed the film-makers room for speculation which De Mille claimed to have been supported by intense research into authentic but not too clearly identified sources.

To prevent the prophesied appearance of a deliverer for the Hebrew slaves in Egypt, the Egyptians decree that all first-born Hebrew children will be killed. The infant Moses (played by Fraser Heston, who was born during production of the film) is cast adrift in a basket on the Nile, but is found and raised in the court of Pharaoh Sethi (Sir Cedric Hardwicke), who treats the child as his adopted son. As an adult, Moses becomes a noted military commander, leading his army to successful conquest of the Ethiopians. But he is also in constant conflict with Sethi's real son Rameses (Yul Brynner). When Moses comes to the defence of a Hebrew slave named Joshua (John Derek), another Hebrew, Dathan (Edward G. Robinson), reveals to Rameses the truth of Moses' origins. Banished, Moses travels far and wide, and marries the shepherdess Sephora (Yvonne de Carlo). He is then urged by Joshua to return to Egypt and free the slaves. Eventually Moses agrees, but only after God has spoken to him, having made His presence known by means of a burning bush.

Moses' return to Egypt involves him with Nefertiri (Anne Baxter), who is married to Rameses but has always loved Moses. For him, Nefertiri betrays Rameses, but this is only a small measure of the problems Egypt suffers through the return of Moses. He brings many plagues down upon the Egyptians before leading his people in search of the Promised Land. Along the way he uses God's power to part the Red Sea and drown their pursuers.

Moses now leads his people to Mount Sinai, which he alone ascends to receive from God the Ten Commandments. During his long absence the freed slaves grow restless and turn to pagan worship, urged on by Dathan, and Moses is forced to lead them on yet again, this time to wander in the desert for forty years until all those who sinned are dead and their purified descendants can pass into the Promised Land. Moses, who cannot enter, goes up into the mountains to meet his God for the last time.

Apart from the rather clumsily imposed eternal triangle of Moses-Nefertiri-Rameses, the basic storyline is played with suitable dramatic fervour and considerable narrative drive, but by present-day standards of film-making, indeed by the standards of the mid-1950s, De Mille's style is dated and rather overblown. The film is mostly well-paced but, again measured by contemporary standards, is occasionally ponderous and could have withstood quite a piece lopping off its three and a half hours' running time.

Visually, the film benefits from excellent photography by Loyal Griggs, who never knew any other life but the movies. He would work on several other Heston pictures, and his skills were recognized by an Oscar in 1953 for *Shane*.

Cecil B. De Mille's dedication to the project was such that he shrugged off a major heart attack to continue filming and although this, the last film he directed, was not as good as some of his earlier work it is hard to imagine anyone else tackling such a project, let alone bringing it off so effectively.

Most of the supporting roles are well played, with Robinson and Brynner being especially effective. Anne Baxter is hampered by having the most artificial role in the film, with dialogue to match. John Derek, however good he might look, was no actor, but he had yet to decide this for himself. His later career as photographer and creator of various artefacts of his own, among them Ursula Andress and Bo Derek, was still some years away.

Charlton Heston's performance, his physical presence and his voice are here all used for the first time to full effect (his voice, recorded and slowed down, was also used as the voice of God). It is difficult to think of any actor working at that time and of his generation – he was just past 30 when production began – who could have played the role with a fraction of his power and dignity. Burt Lancaster brought similar qualities to his portrayal in the Italian TV version in 1975, but by then he had reached the age of 62 and was accepted as a performer of mature roles. In *The Story of Mankind* (1957) the role of Moses was played by Francis X. Bushman, the former silent movie star, who was then 74. It was Bushman who provided the narration for the re-release of Heston's first film, *Peer Gynt*. His career had other similarities to Heston's. He too helped pay his way as a young man by modelling for life classes, and built his career in part upon his striking physical presence; he also worked for Cecil B. De Mille, playing the role of Messala in the original version of *Ben-Hur*, the remake of which still lay ahead of Heston.

Heston's view of his own performance was qualified. As Essoe and Lee record in their study of De Mille, the actor observed that the role of Moses 'was beyond my capacities then, and it would be beyond my capacities now. I dare say it would be beyond Olivier's capacities.'

As Derek Elley reports in his much-needed serious study of the epic film, Heston's opinion of the genre was equally circumspect. 'An epic is the easiest kind of picture to make badly,' he commented, but then acknowledged the central problem by admitting that 'defining an epic is only slightly less complicated than making one'.

Though it may have taken a considerable slice of time from his life, *The Ten Commandments* brought Heston all that it must have promised when the role of Moses was first offered. From this point on, although he would still make films of mixed quality, he was an international star.

The negative aspect of the film was that he would always now be associated in the public mind with the epic, and, moreover, the biblical epic. That his name lingers on in post-biblical consciousness is confirmed in an article by Shyam Bhatia in the *Observer* in 1985. While researching for a tourist's guide to Egypt, the journalist visited a monastery at the foot of Mount Sinai. When asked whether he believed that Moses had come here, a monk replied, 'Haven't you seen the film with Charlton Heston?'

Lydia had been working when her husband started the film, appearing on stage in *The Seven Year Itch* although in an advanced stage of pregnancy. She gave birth to their son, saw him make his first (and last) appearance on film, and was clearly happy to see Chuck back home in the Hollywood hills planning his next project.

Inevitably, *Three Violent People* (1956) was anticlimactic. Any film would have been so at this point in his career, but to a considerable extent this one justified its comparative obscurity with a long catalogue of inadequacies.

An overly complicated tale set in the aftermath of the American Civil War, this has former Confederate soldier Colt Saunders (Heston) warring with just about everyone. He is at odds with government agents who want to take his land; with his one-armed brother Cinch (Tom Tryon) who hates him for, among other things, having had to amputate his arm when they were young; and with his hastily married wife, Lorna (Anne Baxter), who has rather unwisely concealed from her new husband the fact that her last full-time job was as a member of the world's oldest profession.

As Colt has a habit of fighting people who insult his wife, the revelation that she is a former frontier whore makes life more than usually difficult for him. A pillar of stern and unforgiving rectitude, Colt orders her to leave, but he allows her to stay on a while when he learns that she is expecting his child. By the time he has fought off his brother, alienated his Mexican ranch-hands, defeated the government agents and generally faced up to almost as many problems as Moses,

At odds with actor Tom Tryon (later novelist Tom Tryon) in Three Violent People.

Colt softens his heart enough to allow his wife to stay on at the ranch and all ends more or less happily.

With its several strong story threads and a better-than-average script for a routine western, *Three Violent People* appeared to have quite a lot going for it, but it never fully overcomes the shortcomings in direction (Rudolph Maté again), some changes made during post-production, and some wildly over-the-top playing from Miss Baxter, Tom Tryon (who would later exchange a career as a not-very-good actor for one as a first-rate novelist) and various inadequate minor role players including Gilbert Roland, Forrest Tucker and Bruce Bennett (the one-time Olympic swimming champion and the best Tarzan ever to essay the role).

Once again, Heston has a part which comes close to the real man. His character's shell never fully breaks open and therefore matches, in part, those personal characteristics of Heston's which most conflict with the need to reach out to an audience. It is unfortunate that the roles in which these qualities appear, thus allowing him to give a good performance, are only rarely in good productions. Too often, they are in poorly realized films such as *Three Violent People*.

In more ways than one, this film was a come-down for Heston after his work with De Mille, and even the continuing presence of cameraman Loyal Griggs failed to help.

Fortunately for his next role Heston found himself in harness with former *enfant terrible* Orson Welles. It proved to be a fortuitous collaboration.

By this stage in his career, Heston was regularly exercising those clauses in his contracts which gave him script and casting approval. His value to the studios was such that while he did not always have formal approval of the directors for his films, his views were certainly taken into account.

When he heard the name of Orson Welles mentioned in connection with the new film he was being offered, he leapt at the chance to work with such an imaginative and innovative director. In fact, the studio had not been considering Welles as director, but as an actor in the role of the villain of the piece. Heston's comments about Welles, part assumption, part suggestion, led to producer Albert Zugsmith, who was noted for nailing together cheap melodramas, dropping his plans to have a studio hack churn out the film. By hiring Welles to direct, he gave the maker of *Citizen Kane* and *The Magnificent Ambersons* his first directing chore in Hollywood for some years. Typically, Welles promptly wastepaperbasketed the existing screenplay, rewrote it and proceeded to direct *Touch of Evil* (1958) with enormous flair. Although later events were to prove that Zugsmith did not know a masterpiece when one was dropped in his lap, the result was a superbly effective piece of Wellesiana.

Ramon Miguel Vargas, a Mexican narcotics detective, and his American wife Susan (Heston and Janet Leigh) are honeymooning in a small town on the Mexican border when a local millionaire and his girlfriend are blown up by a bomb planted in their car. The local Chief of Police, Hank Quinlan (Welles), takes charge of the investigation; he quickly settles on a small-time Mexican crook and finds evidence to support his suspicions. Mike Vargas discovers that the evidence has been planted by Quinlan, not by any means the first time such a thing has happened in the Chief's remarkably successful career as a crime-buster. For his temerity in questioning Quinlan's probity, Vargas earns the cop's enmity. Quinlan now frames Vargas with the aid of local hoodlum Uncle Joe Grandi (Akim Tamiroff), who also has reason to want Vargas discredited. Grandi sends some of the younger members of his gang to Susan with a fake message that they can help her

Confronting the sweaty menace of director/writer/actor Orson Welles in Touch of Evil.

husband. Instead, she is menaced by them, and eventually drugged and dumped in a brothel, where her discovery is bound to ruin her husband's credibility if not his career. In the meantime, Quinlan has had to eliminate Uncle Joe for fear he will expose his part in the crimes, and Susan is additionally framed for the killing. Mike Vargas is alone against the corrupt cop and the criminals but then Quinlan's assistant, Pete Menzies (Joseph Calleia), discovers evidence that his boss killed Grandi. Although unwilling at first, Menzies eventually agrees to being wired for sound and then helps Vargas trick Quinlan into admitting his guilt. At the last moment, Quinlan realizes what is happening and shoots Menzies, but before he can shoot Vargas, Menzies, who is only wounded, shoots and kills his boss.

Filmed in the Los Angeles suburb of Little Venice, which was created at the behest of an eccentric millionaire, *Touch of Evil*, was lifted above its relatively humble origins by brilliant direction and camera work (from Russell Metty), sharply observed characterizations and dialogue, and uniformly fine performances from all the cast, which features Marlene Dietrich in a cameo role as Tanya, the madame of the local brothel, and Welles's old sidekick Joseph Cotten. Mercedes McCambridge, as a lesbian member of the gang sent to frame Susan Vargas, is quirkily interesting and there are effective, if brief, appearances by Dennis Weaver and Zsa Zsa Gabor.

The work of the principals is most convincing: Akim Tamiroff is slimily repellent beneath an ill-fitting wig and Joseph Calleia, as the conscience-stricken cop, thoroughly enjoys the best role in his long career as a fine character actor.

As the egregiously corrupt Quinlan, Welles, bloated and lowering, exudes sweaty menace in every scene yet manages to extract an element of sympathy from his audience when it is revealed that several years previously his wife was murdered by a Mexican whom he was never able to bring to justice.

As the straight investigator, beleaguered by an uncaring or positively antagonistic populace and also affected by the understated problems of being a Mexican in a racist society, Heston gives an interesting performance. He clearly revelled in the opportunity to play a multi-layered character, and one very different from the kind which usually appears in the sort of movie *Touch of Evil* would doubtless have been in another director's hands.

Welles the scriptwriter gets in several neat observations. After the millionaire has been blown to bits at the start Quinlan questions one suspect and observes to him that an old lady on Main Street picked up a shoe, 'and that shoe contained a foot. We're gonna make you pay for that, boy.' Later, Quinlan asks the brothel-keeper to read his fortune. 'You haven't got any,' she remarks with casual certainty.

The real star turns of the movie come, however, from Welles the director, in which role he is ably assisted by photographer Metty.

The opening scenes are rightly revered and watched with awe by film buffs (and by many lesser film-makers). An enormously long and complex tracking shot makes an immediate statement that this movie is being made by someone who knows all the tricks of the trade and then some, and who is more than capable of startling out of complacency anyone who thinks they've seen it all before. Elsewhere, Welles and Metty use a camera mounted on the car which Heston drives, rigged so that it is the actor who operates the camera. Metty contrived to shoot his daylight scenes without the aid of artificial light, thus giving his images textural qualities often lost by other cameramen who pursued clarity without regard for effect.

The overall effect of the film can scarcely be faulted. As Charles Higham has observed, it is 'a work of total passion, delivered at the volume of an ambulance siren'. Unfortunately, as was so often the case with the work of Welles (and many others who stepped outside the bland norm), the producer had additional scenes shot and inserted, although Heston later stated that these in no way undermined Welles' original concept.

Sadly, American critics were less than impressed. The film was poorly received throughout America but did well in Europe where it won prizes and has attained the status of a classic of the genre (perhaps the last true *film noir*).

Heston's view of the film shifted appreciably. As he was working on it and seeing the dailies, he remarked favourably on its quality when confiding to his diary. Later, when the film was released he decided he didn't like it at all. By the time he published his *Journals*, he had swung round to agree with his original impressions. Seen today, there is little doubt that *Touch of Evil* is one of the best two or three films in which Heston has appeared and it ranks high in the work of its director, Orson Welles.

When Orson Welles died in 1985 he left behind many incomplete film projects and several not even started, however often they might have been spoken or thought about. He had always wanted to make a film version of Shakespeare's *King Lear*. Of this, Heston once remarked that 'if Orson ever gets [it] off the ground, and he wants me to play Gloucester – then I'm available.'

As Orson Welles grew older, the surface equanimity he usually displayed was occasionally ruffled. During an excellent and penetrating interview for BBC TV's *Arena*, in which he ranged far and wide over his career and his thoughts on cinema, there were frequent glimpses of the deep sadness, untinged with resentment, that his years in the wilderness had created. Summing up the industry in which he had struggled for most of his adult life, he observed that it 'is about two per cent making movies and 98 per cent hustling. It's no way to spend a life.'

Although not written with such intent, a line in the script of *Touch of Evil*, uttered by Tanya after Hank Quinlan's death, proved a suitable epitaph. 'He was some kind of man.'

Despite, or perhaps because of, his earlier experiences working in TV, Heston's views of the medium were undergoing change at this time. He considered and rejected an offer to make a TV western series, *Cimarron*, but continued appearing in occasional one-off plays. He made a highly successful version of *Beauty and the Beast* early in 1958, followed closely by *Point of No Return*, in which he was again directed by Franklin Schaffner. Yet he was generally intent on concentrating upon his film work and would gradually ease out of TV for a good many years. It was probably a wise decision. American TV drama, which had been as good as any in the world, began a rapid decline brought about in the main through a combination of censorship and harassment by sponsors who did not want their products to be associated with anything that was in the least contentious.

However, Heston's attitude towards the stage remained unchanged and he continued to seek new works in which to test himself and also to return again to those roles he most enjoyed and wanted to improve upon. Macbeth was one such role and he played the part again at Ann Arbor, Michigan in 1959; he also did *State of the Union* in Santa Barbara, California.

On the big screen, Heston's work with Welles had proved sufficiently enjoyable for him to accept a supporting role in a new western primarily for the chance to work with another director he admired, William Wyler.

Just as Welles was mercurial, Wyler was a slow-moving perfectionist who would take and re-take scenes long after anyone else would have packed up and gone home. Although this was irritating to many actors who worked under him, Wyler's care and attention to detail helped them win Oscars. He also won Academy Awards for himself; by this point in his career he had carried off the Best Director award for both *Mrs Miniver* and *The Best Years of Our Lives*. For Heston, working with Wyler was no great hardship, for he too was a perfectionist. A comment he has made about his work brings together those two qualities which would most endear him to Wyler, his obsession with preparation and his willingness to work hard once before the camera: 'Get it right first, then get it good.' Of Wyler, he remarked. 'Willy's poorest film is good by any other standard.'

The Big Country (1958) is the sprawling story of one man's induction into the ways of the West. Jim McKay (Gregory Peck), a former sea captain, comes to a region known by its residents as the Big Country and falls slap into the middle of a range war between the Terrills and the Hannasseys. As Jim is to marry Pat Terrill (Carroll Baker) he hasn't much choice when it comes to choosing sides. But the fevered animosity of the heads of the two clans, Major Terrill and Rufus

Backing up Charles Bickford in the range war that divides The Big Country.

Hannassey (Charles Bickford and Burl Ives) has so soured Pat that Jim takes up with her best friend Julie Maragon (Jean Simmons). This throws Pat into a relationship with the foreman of the Terrill spread, Steve Leech (Heston), which sets up further conflict, this time between Leech and McKay. The mutual attraction between McKay and Julie serves to alienate further the former seaman from the denizens of the Big Country, for she owns the only patch of land with water, which both Terrill and Hannassey need. When Hannassey kidnaps Julie, McKay follows and meets the old man, with whom he forms a grudging relationship. Eventually, the destructive range war culminates in a shoot-out which kills off the two old men. It is the two pairings, McKay and Julie, Leech and Pat (who has inherited her father's land), who are left to pick up the pieces.

The relative simplicity of the storyline is strengthened by good characterizations and the vision of the land, which emerges superbly in the hands of director Wyler and the brilliant Czechoslovakian-born photographer Franz Planer, who has far more scope here to exercise his talents than he had on his earlier film with Heston, *Bad for Each Other*. The music, by Jerome Moross, helped too; it became the archetypal western movie score, evoking, as it does, all the atmosphere and exhilaration of the wide open spaces conveyed by the film's title.

All acting performances are good, especially those of Charles Bickford and Burl Ives as the warring patriarchs. An authoritative actor, Bickford was an abrasive personality, a quality which gave many of his screen roles an extra dimension. Here he brings to his role a sense of the rugged individualism which was needed by the men who carved out and thereafter ruled vast areas of the American wilderness. Bickford also conveys a suggestion of warmth beneath the surface of his character. (This is a quality which many of the directors with whom he clashed over the years might well have doubted the actor to possess.) Ives was originally best-known as a folk-singer but drifted into films after World War II, where he soon became a reliable portrayer of larger-than-life roles that matched his huge physical bulk. Surprisingly perhaps, for those who are familiar only with his singing, Ives' performance conveys deep wells of suppressed vindictiveness. His voice, squeezed out in a high-pitched nasal whine, drips with barely concealed insincerity. He won the Oscar for Best Supporting Actor for his role as Rufus Hannassey.

Heston's performance in an unsympathetic role is impressive, and he and Peck have some good scenes together. Indeed, the moment when their mutual antagonism boils over into a fist fight provides one of the film's high spots. Imaginatively, Wyler chose to film the scene entirely in long-shot, thus making a statement about the futility of their conflict as the two tiny figures battle it out against the hugely majestic landscape instead of showing it in bone-crunching close-up as almost any other director would have done.

The role Heston played in the *The Big Country* was not one he would normally have been expected to undertake. With all the film's main scenes going to others, his was very much the supporting role which is so often played by very young actors on the way up, or older ones on the way out. As an established leading man, it was a brave decision for him to risk being thought of as either one or the other. His role here was also unusual for him in that while he was not exactly a villain he was far removed from the heroes with whom he was becoming associated in moviegoers' minds. Within the screen space he was given he conveyed the frustrated bitterness of his character as much from his soured expression as from the content of his lines. The fact that the size of the role was such that he could not exert much influence on the film as a whole did not concern him. What mattered was that he could observe the work of a great director at close range.

Although big in scope and visual imagery, *The Big Country* fell well short of being an epic western, even if the writer of a favourable review in the London *Times* was moved to observe that the film 'is not quite an epic, but it is touched with an epic quality.'

Importantly for Heston, he developed a good working relationship with Wyler, something which was to prove enormously beneficial to his career in the very near future.

Before that, however, he returned to a character he had played before, Andrew Jackson, in a movie planned by Cecil B. De Mille but produced and directed by other hands, among them those of Henry Wilcoxon. Originally an actor, Wilcoxon was another star of the silent screen whose career intersected and bore superficial resemblances to Heston's. He had played Mark Antony in Cecil B. De Mille's 1934 version of *Cleopatra* and thereafter worked with De Mille on a number of projects including *The Greatest Show on Earth* and *The Ten Commandments*.

Buccaneer (1958) is another remake from the De Mille canon which was originally made in 1938. This story covers the period of American history known as the War of 1812, which culminated in the Battle of New Orleans. At this time Jackson was a general in the army fighting the British and was obliged to seek assistance from the notorious pirate Jean Lafitte (Yul Brynner). To divert the audience from the implicit history lesson, the sub-plots include a love affair between Annette Claiborne (Inger Stevens) and Lafitte, who breaks off to sink the ship upon which Annette's sister is sailing. Compounding this indiscretion

Old before his (and Old Hickory's) time for The Buccaneer.

by hanging the ship's captain, Lafitte understandably earns the wrath of Annette's father, who happens to be the Governor of Louisiana (E.G. Marshall). The hanged captain's daughter, Bonnie Brown (Claire Bloom), also yearns for the pirate, and it is with her that he eventually sails over the horizon. Before that, however, Lafitte has earned himself a free pardon from General Jackson for his help in defeating the British. Unfortunately, communications being what they were in those days, the climactic battle takes place after the war has ended.

Heston's second fling at Old Hickory conveyed some of the anguish felt by a man obliged to ally himself with pirates in order to defeat his nation's enemies, but it suffered from an entirely uncharacteristic slip, which he made during his customary research for the role. Despite having played Jackson in *The President's Lady* five years earlier, Heston made the mistake of basing his make-up for the new film on a portrait of Jackson painted many years after the events depicted in *Buccaneer*. However, any stiffness incurred by portraying an old man when he should have been relatively young was entirely overshadowed by the even stiffer direction of Anthony Quinn (then De Mille's son-in-law).

Although performing ably enough in all his scenes, whether in action against the British or in equally bitter conflict with his allies, Heston failed this time to make Andrew Jackson a man of the qualities he had suggested in the earlier film. Sometimes querulous, there is never the impression that here was a man who would one day become the President of the United States. Perhaps Heston had hoped for better things when approached to make a film under the De Mille banner. It may be that his disappointment at the way things turned out overcame his dedication to one of his personal heroes.

In the event, *The Buccaneer* was not an auspicious film, but it did mark the end of the contractual agreement Heston had had with Paramount for eighteen films since he first signed with Hal Wallis.

Next came a film that William Wyler had been thinking about while making *The Big Country*, and with it Charlton Heston found himself making his second epic.

Ben-Hur (1959) was a massively budgeted film, and in preparing for it MGM considered several other actors before settling on Heston. In the event, although Heston was not the studio's first choice, Wyler seems to have had few doubts that Heston was the right man for the part and the outcome proved this to have been the right decision.

The story was based upon the novel by General Lew Wallace, a very early entry into the genre of books which set fictional characters into a true historical background. Wallace wrote this novel while representing the United States Government in its attempts to bring peace to the South-west during the range wars in which Billy the Kid played a bloody role. As Governor of the state of New Mexico, Wallace met the Kid in secret in the hope of making a deal; but he failed, and ensuing events have provided material for countless Hollywood westerns.

Ben-Hur is set in Judea at the time of the Roman occupation. Judah Ben-Hur (Heston) is a prince of this land and a close friend of Messala (Stephen Boyd), a Roman soldier presently serving in Judea as a member of the occupying forces. When Messala fails to persuade Ben-Hur to inform on resistance leaders the two men become enemies. Taken prisoner after an accident that is interpreted as an attack on the governor, Ben-Hur is helped by Jesus (Claude Heater), the carpenter from Nazareth, who gives him water despite threats from the Roman officials.

Making a William Wyler movie may be like having a Turkish bath but . . .

. . . in Ben-Hur *Heston was at least adopted by Jack Hawkins.*

Ben-Hur endures two years as a galley slave but saves the life of the consul Arrius (Jack Hawkins) in a battle. Returning to Rome, Arrius helps Ben-Hur and eventually declares him to be his adopted son. By now an accomplished racer of chariots, Ben-Hur nevertheless decides to return to his homeland. Along the way he meets Sheik Ildermin (Hugh Griffith), who asks him to drive his horses in the chariot race against Messala, but Ben-Hur declines: he cannot rest until he has found his mother and sister. Instead, he finds his home occupied by former servants, including Esther (Haya Harareet), who was and is still in love with him.

Ben-Hur calls upon Messala and asks for his help in locating his mother and sister, who have been imprisoned since the day of the so-called 'attack' on the governor. They are discovered to be lepers. On their way to a leper colony, they persuade Esther to tell Ben-Hur that they are dead; she does so, but implies that they were killed years ago on the orders of Messala.

Bitterly angry now, Ben-Hur agrees to drive Sheik Ildermin's chariot at the great circus in Rome, in a race which Messala is determined to win at all costs. During the race, Messala eliminates contestant after contestant, ruthlessly causing destruction and death. Only by the most

On the set with William Wyler, Haya Harareet, Sam Zimbalist and Stephen Boyd during Ben-Hur.

Neck and neck with Stephen Boyd and not a stand-in in sight during the chariot race in Ben-Hur.

skilful and determined driving can Ben-Hur survive, and eventually it is Messala who is thrown to the ground and dragged along before being trampled by the horses of the remaining chariots, vainly pursuing Ben-Hur to the finish. Near to death, Messala tells Ben-Hur that his mother and sister are still alive – in the Valley of the Lepers.

Now militantly opposed to the Roman regime, Ben-Hur joins other resistance fighters but Esther, eager that he should adopt the ways of Jesus of Nazareth, goes to the leper colony to seek his mother. Ben-Hur follows her and is eventually reunited with his mother, Miriam (Martha Scott), and sister, Tirzah (Cathy O'Donnell), who is dying. He takes them to Nazareth, where Jesus is already being tried; they see Him only when He emerges to carry His cross along the Via Dolorosa.

Ben-Hur recognizes Him from the time many years before when this man gave him water. When Ben-Hur tries to help Jesus, he is forced away by Roman soldiers – but not before Jesus has recognized him.

Later, during a storm, Miriam and Tirzah find that they are miraculously cured, a result of touching Christ's cross, and while Ben-Hur and his family rejoice at what has happened the cross standing on the hilltop is revealed to be supporting its human burden no longer.

William Wyler had not previously made an epic film and some of the problems associated with the genre were unfamiliar territory for him. Especially difficult were the crowd scenes, which are not accomplished in the manner in which, say, De Mille might have made them. Nevertheless, Wyler succeeded, as did few other epic directors, in finding a way in which he could encapsulate the spectacular and potentially overwhelming ingredients of the film. He achieved this by developing a tightly observed conflict between two people, in this case Ben-Hur and Messala. The manner in which the chariot race is filmed is a good example of this.

This was shot in part by Wyler and in part by the second-unit director, Yakima Canutt, and his colleague Andrew Marton. Canutt was without equal in the history of Hollywood stuntmen and stunt directors, and his talent was never better demonstrated than here. Despite the spectacle and high drama of the overall event, it is essentially a battle between two individuals representing good and evil. Later, at a seminar held at the American Film Institute's Center for Advanced Film Studies, Wyler discussed *Ben-Hur* with Heston, who at one point underlined this facet of the filming. 'I think what makes [the race] unique is not the remarkable chariot work for which Yakima Canutt was largely responsible, but the fact that the race is photographed and plays on the screen as a conflict between two men.' He also praised Wyler's decision to resist the temptation of using too 'many more of these incredible shots which Yak and Marton made'.

Although only a short section of the overall film, which runs for more than three-and-a-half hours, the race stays in the memory even after other events and the performances have faded. After long and careful tuition from Canutt, Heston drove the chariot in almost all the scenes shot for the film. (In the original version, Francis X. Bushman had also done his own charioteering.) One moment in the race, the spectacular leap where Ben-Hur's chariot leaps over the wreckage of others, was undertaken by Joe Canutt, following skilfully in his father's ground-breaking footsteps.

Not that the actors failed to measure up. Stephen Boyd gave the best

Ben-Hur with sister (Cathy O'Donnell), mother (Martha Scott) and servant-cum-lover (Haya Harareet).

performance of his often lightweight career, Hugh Griffith was bawdily over the top but compulsively watchable (and won the Oscar as Best Supporting Actor), and Jack Hawkins was sturdily effective in a role which, given his second-billing, was surprisingly small. In the title role, Charlton Heston took every opportunity offered to make an impact and never once suffered the indignity which overtakes many actors in epics, that of getting lost in the crowd. This is due in part to his own skills, but he was also aware of the benefits accruing from working with William Wyler. As he observed, 'Doing a film for Wyler is like getting the works in a Turkish bath. You damn near drown but you come out smelling like a rose.'

The female roles were less successful but as none of them is especially significant this does not noticeably weaken the film.

Surprisingly, although not approached by Wyler in the same manner as De Mille would have handled the tale, *Ben-Hur* becomes a much more effective piece of religious film-making. In many scenes there is a real sense of the wonder and awe felt by the people of the time when faced with the turbulent events of the days in which they lived.

Heston's performance in the title role is remarkable among portrayals of epic heroes not only for the fact that he remains visible amidst

Introducing son Fraser to director William Wyler on the set of Ben-Hur.

the excitement and the extras. His physical appearance here carries the requisite conviction even more strikingly than when he appeared as Moses. Quite clearly, his Ben-Hur was a man who *could* have survived the galleys with fortitude; he could rise to the top of a decidedly dangerous profession, as a charioteer; he was a man who would retain his dignity under the most appalling and degrading conditions; and he was also a man who could bend to a religious faith without becoming either soft or a zealot.

True, the scenes with Esther are a shade stiff – but here that customary failing works for him as the characters' relationship, that of master and servant who fall in love, is also awkward. The scenes between Ben-Hur and his mother and sister work well and effectively contrast the hard-edged nature of most other scenes in the film, especially those with Stephen Boyd. That these two characters never display the homosexual shadings allegedly written into the version of the script on which Gore Vidal worked is not really surprising. Had Vidal worked upon the Ramon Navarro version of the film things might have been different, but neither Heston nor Boyd give any hint that they were aware of any such qualities in the script.

In all, Heston's performance was everything that he and those who

63

wanted him for the role can have hoped for; moreover, it gave him money in the bank for a long time to come.

The film's statistics are mind-bending. Filmed at Rome's Cinecittà Studios, the set, which extended to 150 acres, became a major tourist attraction. The circus in which the chariot race takes place was constructed full-size, using hundreds of tons of timber and steel and sand, which was hauled from the beaches – where it presumably went unmissed by the tourists, who were too busy viewing the exciting events at the studios. The stands at the circus eventually supported 8,000 extras, after having first provided a year's work for hundreds of carpenters and other builders. In the end, the effort put into this set, and all the other lavishly furnished sets, proved to have been worthwhile, for the finished film glows with the kind of extravagant production values that were soon to become a thing of the past.

In all, *Ben-Hur*, termed by *Variety* as the 'blockbuster to top all previous blockbusters', was a decided success. Although out of competition, it was chosen to open the Cannes Film Festival, and it also cleaned up at the Academy Awards, where it netted eleven trophies. Apart from the Oscar for Griffith, awards were picked up by, among others, Wyler, photographer Robert Surtees, composer Miklós Rózsa, the movie itself won as Best Picture and Charlton Heston won as Best Actor.

One sad incident occurred on 4 November 1958, when producer Sam Zimbalist visited the set, spoke with several people, including Heston, then went back to his villa, collapsed and died.

Despite the Academy Award and a generally good critical reaction for a film in which he appeared in all but a few minutes of screen time, the impression Heston made was not universal. Later he would delight in telling the tale of the actor Jeff Chandler being stopped in the street by a fan and congratulated on his performance as Ben-Hur. Chandler politely pointed out that he had not been in the film. 'Listen,' the aggrieved fan complained, 'if you're not Burt Lancaster, who the hell are you?'

Such individuals aside, Heston was now even more firmly associated in the public mind as an epic actor and was faced with a period of potential anti-climax similar to that which had occurred after *The Ten Commandments*. In the event, his next three pictures were to be as varied as it was possible to be. A tight-knit thriller, another epic, albeit on a much smaller-scale than *Ben-Hur*, and a light comedy. He was also about to tackle another stage role in his first working relationship with Laurence Olivier, the actor he most admired. He can hardly have expected that this would turn out to be a thoroughgoing disaster.

CHAPTER
Four

'Change is healthy; an actor thrives on diversity.'
Charlton Heston

Heston's 1959 version of *Macbeth* at Ann Arbor was performed during the period when he was working on *The Wreck of the Mary Deare* (1959), in which he co-starred with Gary Cooper. By this time Cooper was a very sick man, but, as Heston has recounted, Cooper did his work uncomplainingly, even though some of it necessitated long hours of immersion in a studio tank used for the underwater work demanded by the story.

Coincidentally, among the movie roles which Heston had been offered some years before but had turned down was one which eventually went to Cooper. The veteran actor's performance in *High Noon* proved to be a high point in a distinguished career. Now the two men shared the only parts of any consequence in this story of salvage and skullduggery at sea. John Sands (Heston) is a marine salvage expert who one foggy night comes upon a ship apparently adrift in the English Channel. On board he finds Captain Gideon Patch (Cooper), who saves Sands' life when he tries to return to his own vessel, an ocean-going tug. After various misadventures, during which Patch runs his ship aground and is subsequently accused of deliberately wrecking her, the two men collaborate in exposing the truth. The ship's owners are behind a plot to scuttle her for the insurance money, having already illegally sold off the cargo at a foreign port. With Patch's name cleared, he grants Sands the opportunity to claim the insurance company's reward.

A simple enough tale, the story probably read better in Eric Ambler's screenplay than it turned out on screen. The characters of Patch and Sands are insubstantial and neither actor is able to make much of them. There is a staginess to the entire film which even the action sequences do little to lift, suggesting that its origins were theatrical rather than in a Hammond Innes novel.

Heston welcomed the chance to work with Cooper, having admired him for many years, if only from a cinema seat. Of Cooper, Heston has observed that he 'projected the kind of man Americans would like to be, probably more than any actor that's ever lived.'

The teeth-gritting determination of the character he is called upon to play here was becoming second nature to Heston. Indeed, some critics felt that the only shading in many of his performances lay in the degree to which he did or did not clench his jaw. Faced with working opposite Gary Cooper, at his best the epitome of the laconic-cowpoke school of acting, Heston could have attempted to match his idol. On balance it is probably as well that he did not, for the throwaway line has never been Heston's forte and he was not yet right for the casual dignity of the weary but not yet beaten man whom Cooper displayed so easily. In his performance as John Sands there are signs that Heston played a deliberate second fiddle to the ailing Cooper. If that is so then it is both understandable and commendable, even if it is not the kind of behaviour that wins acting awards.

With a visibly ailing Gary Cooper on the bridge during The Wreck of the Mary Deare.

Among the largely British supporting cast, which had little to do, was Richard Harris, making only his third screen appearance.

As much as he had enjoyed performing with one of his screen heroes, even more important to Heston was the opportunity to act in a play directed by Laurence Olivier. Staged on Broadway, *The Tumbler* by Benn Levy was a long time in the undertaking but sadly short-lived in production. It closed after only five performances, in February 1960, but Heston would later claim to have no regrets at having passed up a movie with Marilyn Monroe (*Let's Make Love*) in order to do it and to learn more about his craft in the process. At this same time he also refused an offer to make *The Grass Is Greener* with Cary Grant, a role taken instead by Robert Mitchum.

In *The Tumbler*, which is set in England, Heston took the role of Kell, who is attracted to Lennie. For her part, Lennie (played by Rosemary Harris) is in love with Kell but later discovers him to be her stepfather – who has not only been her mother's lover but might even have murdered her father. The unavoidably brooding quality such a theme suggests was not overcome by Olivier's direction. Brooks Atkinson, writing in *The New York Times*, described the first act as 'not only excessively torpid but also intolerably overwritten; and the second act is long and dull.' However, Atkinson continued, 'nothing unkind will be said here about any of the actors. Charlton Heston as the stepfather [is] massive, masculine and fluent.'

Heston's deep love for the theatre has led him to observe the essential differences between the stage traditions of America and those of Britain. America's stock companies, while in some respects matching the long tradition of the provincial repertory theatre in Britain, have not produced the same steady supply of stage actors ready and able to tackle the classics. For a man of Heston's inclinations in the theatre, it has also proved a great handicap to have been forced to fight for the production of all but the surefire Shakespeare plays on American stages. Given his aptitude and his inclinations, to say nothing of his ambitions, it is tempting, if idle, to speculate on how his career might have gone had he been born in England. Of his ability, Olivier once told him that he was sure he could be 'a great actor . . . the only one in America in my time'.

Around this time Lydia Heston's career underwent a major change, for although she was still being offered movie roles she was reluctant to accept them when they clashed with Chuck's work. Eventually, advised by her agent to choose between her career or her husband's, she settled for his. While she would continue to make occasional stage appearances with him, from this point onwards her life would centre upon the home – until ill-health prompted a reassessment and opened up a new career.

However, she turned her frequent trips abroad with her husband to good effect when she contributed an article entitled 'Around the World on 1200 Calories a Day' to the February 1961 issue of *Ladies' Home Journal*.

Although egocentrically concerned with his own career, Heston's comments in his *Journals* reveal that he was not insensitive to the changes he forced, often unconsciously, upon his family, but now, with *The Tumbler* hastily and somewhat ignominiously laid to rest, he continued with his film career and began his third starring role in an epic motion-picture.

Once again, a specific historical place and period were chosen, this time mediaeval Spain. Rodrigo Diaz was a Spanish nobleman of the eleventh century whose life was intertwined with that of King Alfonso VI. Despite the fact that he was married to a noblewoman, Ximena (Chimene), who came from the same family as the king, Rodrigo had problems with Alfonso. Rodrigo, known as *Seid*, meaning lord, fought against invading Moors in defence of the city of Valencia in 1099, but refused the crown of the city, offering it instead to Alfonso who had banished him.

In bringing this story to the screen in *El Cid* (1961), producer Samuel Bronston, director Anthony Mann and screenwriters Philip Yordan and Fredric Frank succeeding in offering on-screen spectacle and grandeur without sacrificing the intensity of the real-life story at the centre of which lie the twin themes of love and honour.

Rodrigo (Heston), whose name of *Seid* evolved into the later Spanish *Cid*, helps his countrymen fight off alien invaders led by Ben Yussuf (Herbert Lom), but his actions are misunderstood and he is brought to trial. When his father is insulted he challenges a nobleman to a duel, kills him and is himself then threatened with execution by his victim's daughter, Chimene (Sophia Loren), with whom El Cid falls in love. The court's deliberations are interrupted by the arrival of more invaders, and El Cid asks to be allowed to challenge the newcomers' champion to single-handed combat as a means of proving whether he is innocent or guilty of the charges of treason which face him. In the encounter El Cid wins, and despite further attempts by Chimene to have him killed he remains in love with her. Commanded by the king to marry El Cid, Chimene agrees but tells her new husband that she still wants revenge and will never live with him as his wife. When the old

Failing to persuade Sophia Loren to wear ageing make-up for El Cid.

king dies his two sons, Sancho and Alfonso (Gary Raymond and John Fraser), fall out. Ben Yussuf, with whom El Cid has earlier been in conflict, has Sancho killed and supports Alfonso's bid for the throne. Humiliated by El Cid, who insists that he declare his innocence in the matter of his brother's death, Alfonso exiles him. Before he leaves, however, El Cid and Chimene are reconciled and she joins him in his banishment.

While Chimene takes refuge in a convent, El Cid fights many battles over the next few years and builds up a strong and faithful following. Then Ben Yussuf attacks Alfonso, who sends for El Cid. Though he initially refuses to intercede, he later changes his mind, telling Chimene, who has now borne him twin daughters, that he must defend Valencia so that the Spanish people can become independent of the many invaders who seek to rule their land. Alfonso then finds Chimene

69

Accepting the cheers but not the crown of Valencia in El Cid.

and takes her and the two girls hostage, but she succeeds in rejoining her husband. El Cid relieves Valencia and is offered the crown, but accepts it only in the name of Alfonso.

Now Valencia is surrounded by Ben Yussuf's massive forces. El Cid decides on a surprise attack, in which he is mortally wounded. Knowing that his people must attack again and this time cannot risk defeat, he asks Chimene to aid him. 'You cannot save my life,' he tells her. 'You must help me give it up.'

Next morning, El Cid's body is strapped, in a riding position, to his horse so that he can ride out beside Alfonso. The enemy forces, having seen the arrow strike what they were sure was a mortal blow, fall back in amazement as El Cid's armour glows with what appears to be heaven-sent light, and are routed.

Anthony Mann's direction is consistently excellent. He is greatly aided by the superb photography of Australian Robert Krasker, who had worked as an assistant on many fine British films including *Henry*

V, The Four Feathers and *The Thief of Baghdad* before taking charge of such films as *Brief Encounter*, *Odd Man Out* and *The Third Man*, for which he won an Oscar. Both Mann and Krasner were helped out by nature on one occasion. While setting up the shot in which El Cid's dead body was to be brought out on horseback, Mann saw a flash of sunlight catch the armour of an extra who happened to be riding by. Hastily they shot the scene, and as the sunlight catches the armour of El Cid it gives it a celestial aura that no amount of carefully rigged artificial light could have matched.

Battling in El Cid, *a better film than even its supporters believe.*

Just as William Wyler had been new to epic spectacle before he took on *Ben-Hur*, so too was Anthony Mann a beginner at this particular facet of the film director's trade. While a sound journeyman, Mann's best work came in a sequence of superb westerns, many of them starring James Stewart, which illuminated the genre in the 1950s. Among them were *Bend of the River*, *The Far Country*, *The Man from Laramie* and, especially good and much underrated, *The Naked Spur*.

Mann's work on *El Cid* has been criticized for failing to display the lavish splendour associated with the epic, but this is unfair. In reality, by paying much greater heed to the central characterizations and treating the action sequences in the best traditions of the western director, he gives the film greater depth than is usually the case while still allowing full and free flow to the battle scenes, which have their own inherent excitement.

In his *Journals*, Heston indicates his general dissatisfaction with Mann's work on the film, going so far as to suggest that better films might have resulted had Mann and Wyler traded places on *El Cid* and *Ben-Hur*. Maybe, but, then, maybe not. A similar supposition could be made about almost any pairing in movies. Heston's conclusion, that with Wyler at the helm *El Cid* might have been the greatest epic ever

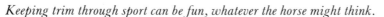

Keeping trim through sport can be fun, whatever the horse might think.

made, cannot be proved either way. In the event, *El Cid* is a much better film than even its supporters appear to think.

There are many fine performances at all levels in the cast list, including such notable British actors as Andrew Cruikshank and Michael Hordern alongside those already mentioned.

In the leading female role Sophia Loren is good, on the whole, and indeed is better than the impression created by reference to Heston's *Journals*. By this time his antipathy towards many actresses was becoming entrenched. Certainly Miss Loren met with his displeasure, whether from repeated late arrivals on set or lack of preparation or simple exhibitions of what might be dismissed as temperament. To a great extent his lack of sympathy for such behaviour is understandable. Anyone who prepares well, arrives on time, hits his marks and knows his lines, and is always highly professional and responsible in his behaviour on the set and in his attitude towards his fellow movie-makers, is entitled to some gripes at anyone who falls short of these high standards. Nevertheless, in a business noted for its highly-strung members and for people whose sense of security is threatened every time a new movie is made and fails, either critically or popularly or financially, to measure up to the last one, or who simply looks in a mirror one day and notices that the face that launched the multi-million-dollar bank balance has developed an extra wrinkle, should be allowed rather more toleration than Heston exhibits.

Then again, Loren's refusal to wear ageing make-up, which left her looking just as young as when the movie started while her screen husband aged by the 20 years the story covered, must have irritated anyone who cares about verisimilitude in movies. Added to this lack of co-operation was Loren's later legal action in suing the movie's makers for having the temerity to put her name below Heston's when *El Cid* was advertised in New York. By any standards, even those of temperamental movie stars, this seems startlingly childish.

A few years later, while flacking for another film, Heston loosed a small broadside against women in movies during an interview with Roderick Mann for the *Sunday Express*. 'By and large,' he said, 'actresses are a different breed of cat. Most of them I wouldn't touch with a pole – or work with where I have some control in the production. It appals and disgusts me, the amateur way most of them treat film-making. The rule of thumb for most of those broads is to be 20 minutes late in the morning and ten minutes late after lunch.' It is a measure of his professionalism that this animosity never shows, yet it may well be that this is one of the root causes of his frequent inability to play a truly emotional scene with a woman.

In the title role of *El Cid*, Heston's performance is of a very high order indeed. The gravity of mien which accompanied his portrayal of Moses and Ben-Hur, his two previous epic roles, remains but is blended with a much deeper and more subtly developed characterization. This role is of a man who is larger-than-life, yet very human; who is powerfully grand, yet humble. It is a difficult balance to bring off but Heston achieves it with remarkable felicity.

The film also benefits from an excellent score by Miklós Rózsa. Most important to its ultimate quality, however, is the combination of the pace of Anthony Mann's handling of the action sequences (aided by Yakima Canutt, who once again managed his second-unit work with dynamic aplomb) and the intrinsic dignity with which Heston invests his role. Almost without seeming to try, this epic, perhaps more than almost any other American epic film ever made, can hardly be faulted on any grounds whatsoever despite its star's reservations. In his study of the genre, Derek Elley calls it a noble cinematic work and comments that it 'is hard to imagine the film without the towering presence of Heston – surely *the* epic presence, an actor, like Olivier, who plays each role straight down the line, giving a film the necessary conviction to underline the rest of the production.'

Heston was also now beginning to make his mark in other activities. In 1960 he was appointed to the board of the Screen Actors' Guild, a body which took a stance on many issues and that was more than somewhat to the right of American politics, although it was not itself overtly political. In 1954 it had nailed its colours to the mast during the agony of the McCarthy witch-hunts by declaring that 'no person who is a member of the Communist Party or any other organization seeking to overthrow the Government of the United States by force or violence can be eligible for membership.' While not of itself untoward, what is surprising is that the members of the board of SAG at that time thought it necessary to make the statement. After all, strictly speaking, anyone who didn't measure up to that credo was by inference a traitor. Such individuals should have been, and at that time were being, dealt with by the authorities (along with thousands who were merely thought to be traitors or who simply refused to bow the knee to often self-serving government committees). Seeking membership of SAG would surely have been fairly low on any list of such a person's priorities. The statement has instead all the hallmarks of an organization plaintively pleading, 'Look at me, I'm clean.'

Contrasting with SAG's image of the time was Heston's own political stance. Admittedly low-profile, he was deeply concerned over Civil

Rights issues and in 1963 campaigned over discrimination against black actors in Hollywood. Even earlier, before such issues became front-page news, he dismissed his involvement in a demonstration against segregated restaurants in Oklahoma City by remarking to the *Guardian*, in 1961, that such action 'was easy for me to do because I didn't stand to lose much over it'. In 1963 he was no longer in a minority when he joined many other fellow actors, and tens of thousands of concerned fellow Americans, for the March on Washington which culminated in Martin Luther King's 'I have a dream' speech.

In any event, Heston's involvement with SAG began at a time when other factors were exercising the board. Conflict with the studios led to a month-long actors' strike in 1960, and from this time on, for many years, he was heavily involved with SAG. He became a vice-president at the end of 1961 and was eventually appointed president, in 1963, an office he held for several terms.

Heston had not entirely abandoned television work. By this time live drama had virtually disappeared. *The Fugitive Eye* about a one-eyed carnival man, in which he appeared in 1961, was filmed in advance of transmission. Two years later he played Thomas Jefferson in *The Patriots* for NBC, the third of his portrayals of American presidents.

Domestically, he and Lydia and their young son, Fraser, made regular trips back to Michigan and their home near St Helen. (His own production company was named the Russell Lake Corporation.) It was in August 1961 that the Hestons increased their family by adopting a little girl named Holly Ann.

The happiness of his private life did not, unfortunately, shine through into the comedy film that Heston now made, only his second such essay. Very much the work of Melville Shavelson, who produced, directed and scripted the film, *The Pigeon That Took Rome* (1962) proved to be one of those movies which must have looked a whole lot better in advance of a camera being turned than it did from that moment on. (Shavelson also had problems with another movie, *Cast a Giant Shadow*, about which he wrote a very funny account in *How to Make a Jewish Movie*. In another book, a novel entitled *Lualda*, Shavelson took his life in his hands when he wrote about the rise of an Italian actress in a manner which must have kept Sophia Loren's lawyers up all night trying to figure if they should sue.)

The Pigeon That Took Rome tells the story of two American soldiers, Paul MacDougall and Joe Contini (Heston and Harry Guardino), who enter Rome ahead of the advancing Allied armies in order to spy on

Taking tips on priestly behaviour from Harry Guardino in The Pigeon That Took Rome.

German troop emplacements. They plan to send reports back by carrier pigeon, but the Italian family with whom they shelter cooks most of the birds and eats them. They steal replacement birds but discover, too late, that these homers are trained to return to German lofts – which causes more than a few problems. All turns out well in the end with the two soldiers marrying the daughters of their Italian hosts while the one pigeon that survived the earlier feast does its job and wins a medal. The film does not linger over the intriguing problem of just where you pin a medal on a pigeon.

As observed earlier, Heston was by no means inept at playing comedy, but this time he failed to rise to the occasion: possibly it was a matter of script, or maybe simple unease at the always problematical subject of being funny in wartime. Certainly he did not find the key to the character he was portraying. Whether in uniform or disguised as a priest, he was always too commanding a figure to have escaped detection, and much too tense for the essentially trivial nature of the part and the film itself.

The film passed unremarked which is, perhaps, unfortunate because it seems to have written off for ever any possibility of Heston making comedies.

His next film, although high drama set amidst the volcanoes and lush landscapes of Hawaii, also failed to ignite audiences. *Diamond Head* (1962) delves into racist bigotry, but without the insight such a subject needs.

Richard Howland (Heston), a rich planter, although romantically involved with Mei Chen (France Nuyen), is angered by his sister's decision to marry a native-born Hawaiian, Paul Kahana (James Darren). The girl, Sloan (Yvette Mimieux), throws an engagement party at which Mei Chen's brother attacks Howland but kills Paul instead. Blaming her brother for this, Sloan runs away but is later found by the dead man's brother, Dean (George Chakiris), who cares for her. Then Mei Chen dies while giving birth to Howland's son. When he refuses to accept the child into his family Sloan and Dean, who plan to marry, step in. Eventually, Howland allows the child to bear his name and accepts the Hawaiian as his brother-in-law.

Once again no one comes out very well, and Heston was stonily uneasy in most of his scenes. Actors are supposed to immerse themselves in their roles regardless of what they think of the characters they are playing, but as has been suggested this is often a problem for Heston. In several respects this must be seen as a criticism of his acting style, yet there must come a point in the careers of all but a few actors where the degree of immersion must take account of personal attitudes. Heston's private life has always been so unfailingly correct that when faced with a role which required him to wholly oppose his own standards he becomes noticeably edgy. In a role such as that of Richard Howland it is probably of no great significance, although it has undoubtedly proved detrimental in more important parts.

He was much happier with his next role, his fourth epic, although on a relatively minor scale, and one which, like so many films, was clearly an exciting prospect at the outset.

55 Days at Peking (1962) was dreamed up by Samuel Bronston, who wanted to follow up his previous collaboration with Heston. So enthusiastic was he that when Heston turned down *The Fall of the Roman Empire* he postponed plans to make that movie and set about turning the half-built sets into a remarkably good facsimile of Peking at the beginning of the twentieth century. With the direction in the hands of Nicholas Ray, a dynamic film-maker whose work was always notable for the individuality he brought to even the most mundane of screenplays, this film held a great deal of promise which was ultimately unfulfilled.

Set in China in 1900, the time of the Boxer Rebellion, one of the aims of which was to rid China of 'foreign devils', *55 Days* tells the story of a major in the US Marines, Matt Lewis (Heston), who finds himself helping defend the embassies of several nations against the Chinese rebels. These rebels are, in fact, closely linked with the Imperial Government of China, and especially with Prince Tuan and the Dowager Empress Tzu Hsi (Robert Helpmann and Flora Robson). Most of the ambassadors had wanted to leave ahead of the Rebellion but are shamed into staying by the determination of the British Ambassador, Sir Arthur Robertson (David Niven), to hold on until the arrival of the British navy.

On his arrival in Peking, Lewis clashes with the Boxers, who are subjecting a priest to water torture during which the man dies. Lewis's life is saved during this incident when his sergeant, Harry (John

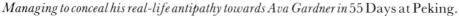
Managing to conceal his real-life antipathy towards Ava Gardner in 55 Days at Peking.

Ireland), shoots a Boxer who is taking a bead on the major. In the comparative comfort of the hotel Major Lewis meets and is attracted to the Russian baroness Natalie Ivanoff (Ava Gardner), who is desperate to leave before the trouble starts in earnest. When Lewis and the German Ambassador (Frederick Pohl) both humiliate Prince Tuan at a grand ball, the Chinese nobleman is determined to be revenged. Later, Lewis witnesses a gang of Boxers murder the German. In a demonstration of her honour, the Empress has the gang beheaded in a mass-execution.

As trouble boils up Lewis and his marines help man the barricades around the embassy district, but they are massively outnumbered. The Baroness helps out at the hospital as casualties mount. Among the dead is Lewis's second-in-command, Andy Marshall (Jerome Thor), whose daughter by a Chinese woman is now orphaned. The girl, Teresa (Lynne Sue Moon), now has no hope of ever getting to America, which is where her father had promised to take her. When the beleaguered garrison learns that the relief column has had to turn back, Lewis and his men disguise themselves as Chinese and try to blow up the armoury in the Palace, but are only partially successful. For their part, the Chinese prove highly inventive by bringing up a tower which serves as a rocket launcher. This looks like turning the balance but thanks to a bright idea from Father de Bearn (Harry Andrews) the tower is destroyed.

Eventually, after the Baroness has succumbed to a mortal wound, and the foreigners have held out for 55 days, the Chinese run away as the relief column finally arrives. As Lewis and his men prepare to march out of Peking, Teresa looks on hopefully. At the last moment, Lewis hoists her on to his horse and they leave together.

Unlike *El Cid*, the previous film of Bronston's in which Heston starred, *55 Days* does not really come off. The hastily adapted set is superb. Built in Spain, it really is a full-size city and does not suffer from the occasional anomalies which arise with even the best miniature sets. The action sequences, directed by Yakima Canutt, are uniformly excellent and exciting. Very little else can be said in favour of the film, although how much of this is a result of the massive coronary which Nicholas Ray suffered during filming is hard to assess. Second-unit director Andrew Marton filled the breach until Guy Green, who had made *Diamond Head* with Heston, arrived to complete the film (remaining uncredited). Green was a little more experienced than Ray in this type of film but lacked the American's flair and spare imagery.

Driven by the need to make up time lost by Ray's heart attack and by occasional outbursts of temperament from Ava Gardner, Heston worked almost continuously for three weeks, alternating between day and night scenes until the work was done.

Despite the efforts of all participants to make up for the delays the end result was not what it should have been. The standard of acting suffers both from being submerged in events and from the fact that several important roles were inadequately developed in the screenplay. There is also an uneasy dichotomy in the central premise that audiences should empathize with rampant colonialists.

It may be that the lack of a relaxed atmosphere during the film's making was a contributory factor. This stemmed from antipathy felt by Heston towards Ava Gardner, who comes in for a fearful drubbing in his *Journals*. Her unpunctuality, mingled with several displays of big-star high-handedness, must have militated against the sort of atmosphere in which ensemble film-making flourishes.

As the grimly determined Marine officer, Heston looks the part and conducts himself with appropriate heroics in the action sequences. The great failing of the role is that there is never any suggestion of where this man comes from, nor of where he will go in the end. If he has any life outside this film it does not show through in the screenplay and neither does it emerge in Heston's characterization. As written it is a two-dimensional part; as acted it remains so, and the film is the weaker for it.

Heston's next screen role was a cameo appearance in *The Greatest Story Ever Told* (1965), in which he plays the part of John the Baptist. Overall, the film suffers from religiosity. Neither was it helped by the decision to cast big-name actors in several cameo roles similar to Heston's. With David McCallum, Telly Savalas, Shelley Winters, Sidney Poitier and Van Heflin among a total of perhaps a dozen, much of the audience's boredom was allayed by guessing which star would pop up next. Of all these cameos, John Wayne's appearance as a Roman soldier at Golgotha was the final nail in the cross.

This cameo was Heston's second and last appearance in a biblical epic. For his next film, Heston returned to that great American storehouse of scripts, the Old West, this time for a Civil War drama which had a fair chance to become a truly great western – but sadly never made it.

Directed by Sam Peckinpah, *Major Dundee* (1965) concerns a Union officer, Amos Dundee (Heston), who is playing out the final months of the war as shepherd to a motley gang of Confederate prisoners,

Heston and Sam Peckinpah figure out ways to avoid going over budget on Major Dundee.

criminals and disaffected blacks, formerly slaves but now an unwanted and despised unit of the Union army. On discovering that a Union cavalry post has been attacked by Apaches and the garrison either killed or, in the case of some children, kidnapped, Dundee sets out in pursuit of the Indians after first gaining the word of honour of his senior prisoner and pre-war friend Confederate Captain Ben Tyreen (Richard Harris) that he will assist and make no attempt to escape. Tyreen reluctantly agrees and his men concur with equal absence of relish.

The Indians cross the border into Mexico and Dundee follows, even though he has no authority there; in any event, the Mexicans have problems enough of their own due to conflict with France and their puppet, the Austrian Emperor Maximilian. Dundee's problems are intensified when his party frees a Mexican village from French troops and he has to take on an additional role as protector to various Mexicans and Teresa Santiago (Senta Berger), the Austrian-born widow of a Mexican doctor, whose charms immediately add to the tensions between himself and Tyreen. These tensions are exacerbated by the behaviour of one of Tyreen's men, O.W. Hadley (Warren Oates), who deserts temporarily. Fulfilling an earlier threat, Dundee prepares to execute him; but Tyreen does the job for him, thus rendering implacable the Southerner's hatred for the Northern major.

After a brief dalliance with Teresa, Dundee is wounded by an arrow and enters into a period of self-disgust that he has allowed himself to slip from his previous standards of decency. These standards are, in fact, a puritanical inability to bend to his natural desires, and he now takes to the bottle and the whores of a small town. Eventually, the Indians stop running and attack, but the combined forces of Dundee and his prisoners fight them off and the Apache is defeated. As Tyreen and Dundee prepare to fight a duel of honour, French troops arrive and they have to retain their uneasy truce a while longer. In the battle with the French, Tyreen is killed and afterwards Dundee and a handful of survivors return to the United States.

Unlike almost any other of the 800 or more films which deal with or touch upon the American Civil War, *Major Dundee* is a fascinating and complex mass of conflicting emotions, religious and patriotic beliefs, shifting friendships and enmities, uneasy alliances, temporary allegiances born of convenience, racial bigotry (Dundee treats the Indians, the blacks – for whom he is theoretically fighting this war – and the Mexicans with contemptuous distaste) and Freudian sexual behaviour.

Dallying with beautiful widow Senta Berger in Major Dundee.

The screenplay, by Peckinpah, Harry Julian Fink and Oscar Saul, is a richly woven fabric which suffers only from late changes made by the producers. The latter is a seemingly permanent feature of Peckinpah's work, but this instance was by no means as bad as has often been the case. The ensemble playing is of a very high standard and individual performances stand out, among them Oates as the shiftless but essentially honest deserter, Ben Johnson, a stalwart of many western movies, James Coburn as a one-armed scout and R. G. Armstrong as the Reverend Dahlstrom, a bloodlusting preacher.

Among the changes made by the studio are the defeat of the Indians and the survival of Dundee and less than a dozen of his men, neither of which were conclusions Peckinpah wanted. Some other changes requested by the studio during filming, when it was discovered that the picture was behind schedule (and hence over budget), were resisted by Peckinpah with Heston's backing. The studio bowed to this pressure, presumably on the grounds that they could replace the director but to replace the star would prove disastrously expensive. Later, as an act of contrition at breaking a lifelong rule against being difficult during filming, Heston offered to forgo his fee. It was an offer the producers could not afford to refuse.

In common with many of Peckinpah's films, much of the director's work on *Major Dundee* was either misunderstood or misjudged, and to some extent still is. As it stands, and Heston himself has indicated that the changes made by the studio in this instance did not alter the essence of the director's intentions, *Major Dundee* is still a fine film. It is also an important film in the history of the western, in the work of its director, and in the career of its star.

Much more complex than almost any other role he has played, Major Dundee was obviously absorbing for the actor. All the shadings within Dundee, the equivocation of the character's motivation, the bitterness coupled with despair, and almost suicidal self-disgust, are fluently observed by Heston. That some of the finer points are lost in the unevenness caused by the changes made to the film does not detract from a highly commendable interpretation. Heston's portrayal goes a long way towards allaying the frequent criticism that he is unable to get inside a character. Amos Dundee is a very real man and all the better for his flaws; Heston comes out of the movie a better actor for having made it.

During post-production of *Major Dundee*, Heston celebrated his 41st birthday and could now fairly be said to be in the prime of his career, an international star, and by most standards a rich man. He was also

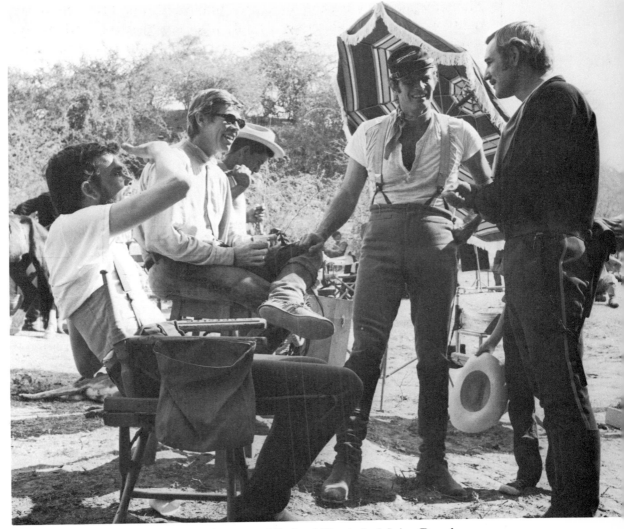

On location with Jim Hutton, James Coburn and Richard Harris for Major Dundee.

firmly entrenched in the popular mind as an epic actor, although he had made only four, more than half his eventual total. His total number of films now stood at 28, including cameo and amateur appearances, which was also about halfway to his present total. His ability to spot a good role remained undimmed, although the quality of the films in which he chose to appear continued to be decidedly suspect.

Immediately in view, however, was the release of a film he had made without taking a break after finishing *Major Dundee*. This was the story of the man whose sculpture of Moses had so resembled Charlton Heston that he had been first choice for the role of the ancient Lawgiver. The man was the artist Michelangelo.

CHAPTER
Five

'He must have grown through sheer tenacity.'
Rex Harrison

The fact that Charlton Heston had begun his Hollywood career with a contract allowing him far more flexibility, and control, over his films than any other actor of his generation (save only, perhaps, Marlon Brando) should have meant that he never made a poor film. Unfortunately, that is not the way things worked out. The first fifteen years saw as many artistic and box-office duds as were made by those actors who were herded by uncaring studios into routine projects. Heston's careful preparation for his films, whether in background research for the characters or simply ensuring that he walked on to the lot on the first day of shooting bang on time and with all his lines learned, did not guarantee quality. Given this measure of care and attention, it must be assumed that when it came to choosing a movie, or his role in it, his judgement was at fault.

Partially to blame for the problem may be the fact that, physically and temperamentally, he was unsuited for many, if not most, contemporary roles. More significantly, the public was not prepared to accept him in such parts. As he observed in an interview with Andrew Lorenz for *The Scotsman*: 'Paul Newman . . . has become the quintessential urban twentieth-century American male [whereas] I have always been regarded as faintly out of place . . . though I don't feel out of place doing those parts. I guess that has to do with the "shadow"; every actor is followed by a lengthening shadow of the audience's memory of all the parts they've seen him play and for me . . . it doesn't include many significant twentieth-century parts.'

Another factor which inevitably influences any actor's choice of roles is, of course, that he can choose only from those which he is offered, together with those that he can produce for himself. Given the enormously time-consuming problems which surround film production, not very many of the latter are possible in the lifetime of any man who is actor first and producer, at best, a poor second.

In Heston's case there is also the fact that during his rise to international stardom, big movies on big screens were very much the order of the day as the last of the Hollywood moguls sought to fend off the (largely imagined) threats of TV and other insidious alternatives to what they had to offer in the way of entertainment. With screens stretching the width and height of the biggest cinemas, actors, too, had to be larger-than-life, and there were precious few in that mould around at the time. There had been a shift, gradual at first but later a stampede, towards naturalistic acting as the Method was widely adopted. Unfortunately, the Method was often downgraded in the public's eyes by actors of limited talent who appeared to think that shuffling and scratching their way across the screen would somehow turn them into a Brando or a Wallach. The contrast between giant movies with roles that demanded massive screen presence and the often insubstantial actors who were available left a large hole into which Heston fitted admirably.

Additionally, there was the undoubted ego-booster of fitting into another kind of gap. As he observed, 'There's a special excitement in playing a man who made a hole in history large enough to be remembered centuries after he died.' Allied to this was the tactile pleasure he undoubtedly felt in checking in his tin-suit for a while. He remarked on one occasion, 'After spending all of last winter in armour it's a great relief to wear costume that bends.'

Combining a flexible costume with a man of historic stature, he now agreed to tackle the role of perhaps the greatest artist of the Italian Renaissance.

Asked by a journalist if he didn't think he was too tall to play Michelangelo, Heston replied, 'No, I think I'm too small.' For any actor with a well-developed ego, and very few do not carry such a burden around with them, this remark suggests a remarkable humility. In this instance, given Heston's high regard for the arts and for artists of the calibre of Michelangelo there is no doubt that he meant what he said.

Apart from all other considerations, the role of Michelangelo must have introduced an element of kinship, for it was another example of Heston's physical appearance matching that of the character he played (in this instance, height apart). Just as he bore a strong facial resemblance to Michelangelo's Moses, he was also remarkably like the real artist, even to the broken nose. By the time the make-up department had accentuated the break, the resemblance was startling.

As with all his roles, Heston went deeply into the artist's life and additionally learned all that he could about the way in which sculptors and painters work. Ultimately, however, Heston's physical similarities, the undoubted sincerity of all participants and the highly effective technical resources put into the film failed to make *The Agony and the Ecstasy* (1965) the major motion-picture experience it should have been.

Michelangelo is urged by Pope Julius II (Rex Harrison) to create a truly unique work of art, the painting of the ceiling of the Sistine Chapel. Unwilling to acquiesce, partly because he has now moved on from being the most acclaimed fresco painter and now prefers instead to sculpt, the artist refuses the Pope's commission. The architect, Bramante (Harry Andrews), is not disturbed, believing that Raphael (Thomas Milian) will do the job equally well, but the Pope is determined to have Michelangelo work on the ceiling. As the Pope is prepared to back up his demand with force, for this was a time when the Vatican had to defend itself vigorously if it hoped to survive, Michelangelo goes into hiding after destroying his first attempts at a design which is not to his satisfaction. The Contessina de Medici (Diane Cilento), with whom Michelangelo has previously had a love affair, is also insistent, but she urges that he should do what his heart dictates. Then, inspired by the natural beauty of the heavens, Michelangelo agrees, although the Pope's intention to hang him if he does not comply with his wishes cannot have been far from his mind.

He begins work, having first constructed a special scaffolding which will allow him to work within a few inches of the ceiling, albeit lying flat on his back. This structure is made of wood and is surprisingly rickety for a man of Michelangelo's technical competence. Later, when the Pope's men try to break it up for kindling during a battle, the artist begs that he be left alone. By this time, the inspired artist has overcome his earlier reluctance and is determined to complete his masterwork. In contrast with the artist's surge of determination, the Pope is now under great pressure as his fortunes go into decline. Soon it is Michelangelo who must inspire Julius to cling on to his faith. Eventually, after years of dedicated and almost crippling work, the painting is completed and the two men, the artist and the warlike man of God, celebrate their achievement.

Battle scenes apart, *The Agony and the Ecstasy* is a very wordy film,

Preparing to paint a masterpiece for The Agony and the Ecstasy.

Asking Rex Harrison what he thinks of it so far, in The Agony and the Ecstasy.

with painter and Pope philosophizing to one another often at interminable length. The screenplay, by Philip Dunne from Irving Stone's novel, frequently overlooks that hoariest of truths, that one picture is worth a thousand words. In this instance, given that the picture is the ceiling of the Sistine Chapel the ratio should have been substantially increased.

The techniques used to recreate a full-size replica of the ceiling are quite remarkable. The real ceiling has faded and cracked and so, using photographs of it, new images in the full brilliance of the original colour were transferred to the movie set. Once completed, the ceiling was then painted over so that the actor could start work on a blank surface. As he worked at his painting the surface cover was gradually removed giving the impression that the work was being created on-camera. It was an example of movie-making skills (in this instance at the Dino de Laurentiis studios in Rome) at their very best.

For much of the film's running time the screen is filled with Michelangelo wrestling with either his ceiling or with the Pope. The performances of the two principals are, therefore, essential to the film's success and for the most part they work, although neither one entirely breaks down that invisible curtain of disbelief which lies between audience and screen.

The two actors appear to have had a wary regard for each other. In an editorial comment in his *Journals* Heston remarked of Harrison that he had 'the temperament of a thoroughbred racehorse . . . highly strung, with a tendency to snort and rear and kick at the starting gate'. For his part Harrison, in his autobiography, observed that 'Heston very politely and very nicely made me feel that it was extremely kind of me to be supporting him.' Harrison also tried to enhance his height, already over six feet, so that he could look Heston in the eye. Without telling his co-star, he had the wardrobe department give him lifts for his shoes (hidden beneath his Pope's robes), but even this failed. 'As the film went on, however, it seemed to me that he was growing. Eyeball to eyeball he was once more a couple of inches taller than I. He must have grown through sheer tenacity.'

The intensity of the character he plays here comes through in Heston's performance, although he does not wholly convince that this was the way in which Michelangelo really behaved. Artists, especially those who work alone, have always proved problematical for moviemakers; the screen appears to need something more tangible than inner compulsion. Heston's inability to internalize a role is more obviously on display here, in his attempt to characterize a man driven almost entirely by inner demons. Given that the story is fictionalized fact, both screenplay and performance can be excused some of their lapses; both, however, would have been better for scenes showing Michelangelo involved in the everyday activities that even great artists must carry out in order to survive in society.

Critical response was muted and the public divided. The inherent suspicion which has attended any attempt by the motion-picture industry to offer 'art' to the mass audience took its toll. In this instance, the creation of a painting which took years to complete, the effort of both the artist and his latterday imitator, to say nothing of the expense of the recreation, failed to impress as much as the film's makers doubtless hoped.

As Charlotte Chandler has recorded, soon after the film's completion Heston was approached by Groucho Marx, who remarked, 'You could have saved a lot of money if you'd painted the Sistine Chapel floor instead of the ceiling.' Although blessed with a lively sense of humour, Heston, understandably, was not amused.

For his next film Heston was once again delving into history. This was for a story based upon a stage play, *The Lovers*, by Leslie Stevens. Brought to the screen as *The War Lord* (1965), the tale is essentially a love story, set amidst the wars between the barbarians and the Normans in eleventh-century Europe.

Chrysagon (Heston), a knight in the service of the Duke of Normandy, is appointed to rule over an area of dankly bleak land, edged to the west by the North Sea. In accordance with the dictates of the times,

Daughter Holly Ann is unsure whether she or the bird is for lunch. On the set of The War Lord.

Chrysagon exercises his *droit de seigneur* when a beautiful peasant girl, whom he has already met and admired, is married. But after being obliged to spend her wedding night in this manner, Bronwyn (Rosemary Forsythe) finds she is in love with the War Lord and he with her. Understandably angered by this turn in events of which they already disapprove, the villagers revolt and attack Chrysagon's castle. This uprising occurs just as barbarian hordes are about to attack. Unable to call upon the peasants for aid, the War Lord is helped only by his fellow Normans. These include his brother Draco (Guy Stockwell), who is already at odds with Chrysagon's flaunting of the codes and traditions by which the family has lived for generations, and the War Lord's cynically pragmatic squire, Bors (Richard Boone). Eventually, Chrysagon overcomes the invaders, but only after he has sustained a fearful wound and is left alone with Bronwyn.

Under the direction of Franklin Schaffner, with whom Heston had worked on TV on a number of occasions in the past, *The War Lord* is very different from the usual epic film; indeed, in many respects it fails to qualify for this generic term. Before being mangled by the studio executives, Schaffner's film was in deliberately stylized form, evoking much of the age of primitive belief and superstition in which the tale is set. In this, the director was aided by superb photography from Russell Metty (with whom Heston had worked on *Touch of Evil*). The misty landscapes, subtly lit, convey the part-natural, part-mystical feeling the film's makers obviously wanted.

The central love story is handled with considerable sensitivity from the moment of the first meeting between Chrysagon and Bronwyn, where she bathes naked in a pool while he looks down on her from horseback, through a gradual reversal of their symbolized roles as he lies wounded, until they eventually establish equality in their mutual love and respect. Given the title of the original work, it is not surprising that their love affair should be so important to the story; what *is* surprising is the fact that the film's makers retained it to such good effect. Too often in movies set in mediaeval times, there has been more than a suspicion that Hollywood could not quite bring itself to believe that men and women of those far-off times had similar emotional responses to their twentieth-century counterparts.

The acting is strong in all roles, with Richard Boone especially fine among the supporting players. Heston's War Lord is at least on a par with his earlier film roles and in its subtlety displays many facets lacking in previous epics.

The screenplay undoubtedly helped. Co-written by John Collier and Millard Kauffman, it had been in the works for a long time. Heston's *Journals* comment on the problems which beset a writer faced with accepting that, unlike almost any other form of creative writing, a motion-picture screenplay is not a solitary activity but one which demands collaboration and co-operation. That this is possibly as much through tradition as necessity does not diminish the need for a writer to give ground in many areas. Collier appears to have had problems in accepting this, but in the event the result was worth the traumas. Responsibility for the fact that the finished film was less than it should have been must lay at the doors of the studio executives who made post-production changes. Certainly it was not the fault of any of the creative participants in its making.

Among those with whom Heston was reunited on this film was Joe

Writing up his Journals *during the filming of* The War Lord.

Canutt, who handled the action sequences in a manner which was doubtless warming to his famous father's heart. Heston rarely uses doubles (there can't be too many people around of his build) and most of what is seen on screen here really is him. A scene in which Heston is engaged in a sword fight with Canutt is particularly memorable.

Also well played are the love scenes – not usually Heston's strongest suit owing to his natural dislike of exposing his feelings. This does not stem from a rooted objection to such scenes for their own sake: he has observed to one interviewer that he certainly does not want to make all his films for his little daughter.

Among the actors playing minor roles in *The War Lord* were Henry Wilcoxon as the Frisian King and Maurice Evans as a priest. Wilcoxon had been associate producer on two of Heston's films and producer on one while Evans, who had enjoyed a long and successful stage career in Britain and America, had starred in the very first professional stage play Heston saw as a young man.

One of his best working relationships with an actress was with Rosemary Forsythe in The War Lord.

But in the end it is Heston's picture. As remarked above, the qualities of his performance are well conveyed in his scenes with Rosemary Forsythe (in itself unusual for one so frequently criticized for failing to work comfortably with women). Such softening of the facade helps make Chrysagon much more of a man than many epic heroes would appear to be. Yet when called upon to play the hero, Heston does this as well as always. Overall his performance has greater texture than is often the case in such films.

In the mid-1960s, Heston made what was to be his last TV appearance for some time, playing Essex in a play which dealt with the uneasy relationship between Queen Elizabeth I and the Earl of Essex. He also performed in the theatre in a role which had long fascinated him and which he dearly wanted to act on screen too: Sir Thomas More in Robert Bolt's *A Man for All Seasons*. He first played More in 1965 in Chicago and then again the following year in Miami and Los Angeles, where audiences and critics were enraptured. It was by now traditional for Lydia to co-star with him in his stage plays, and on this occasion she played the role of More's wife. When the film came to be made the role went to Paul Scofield; Heston's *Journals* reveal his disappointment.

Heston's work with the Screen Actors' Guild greatly increased for his six successive terms as president, and he was also appointed to the National Arts Council. These appointments required him to testify regularly before Senate committees on the arts in general and on the movies in particular. As president of SAG he also thought it necessary to react to union activities in other lands. In August, 1966 he wrote to the *Guardian* newspaper in England, attacking Frank Cousins's decision to use his parliamentary seat to represent the members of his union, the Transport and General Workers', rather than the electorate of his constituency. Elaborating upon the *Guardian*'s use of Edmund Burke as a frame of reference, Heston wrote that the Burke aphorism 'most precisely appropriate to Mr Cousins's shabby solution to his problem [is] "Your representative owes you not his allegiance only, but his judgement. He betrays you, instead of serving you, if he sacrifices it to your opinion".' Some years later, after he had ceased to be president of SAG, Heston was to become deeply involved in a bitter conflict with his successor in an affair to which he would apply much the same principle.

In 1966 Heston made a trip to Vietnam under the auspices of the USO (United Service Organization). As he could neither sing nor dance to entertain the troops, he settled for travelling alone to forward positions there to talk to soldiers and take from them messages which he would relay, personally, to relatives back home. His views on American involvement in Vietnam as expressed in his *Journals* appear mildly hawkish, but this was probably how most Americans felt at this time. Later, however, as many became doves, he appears to have hardened in his view. The following year he went back to Vietnam again. In an editorial comment appended to his *Journals* at the time of their publication (by which time the war was over), he declared that America's greatest fault had lain in its inability, having once made the decision to go in, to win the war quickly and thus minimize the loss of life. Although showing consistency, this is not a view many shared, at least until the mid-1980s when, in the wake of Ronald Reagan's aggressive views on world politics, America again began to think tough.

Sadly, the mid-1960s also brought the death of Heston's father. After a long illness Russell Whitford Carter died on 1 September 1966 while his son was in the air on his way back to Los Angeles after visiting the old man at his home in Detroit.

Back in mid-summer 1963 Heston had expressed his unwillingness to become involved with another epic film. However, he had been impressed by the quality of one particular script and eventually decided to accept another leading role in such a film.

Khartoum (1966) is the story of the final months in the life of General Charles 'China' Gordon, one of the British army's most respected heroes. In casting an American actor to play the role of Gordon, the film's makers were taking a big chance with the British market. They must have been optimistically aware of Charlton Heston's practice of researching his roles with obsessive thoroughness, yet, even so, there was still the matter of the accent, an area where Hollywood had displayed apparent deafness for many years (just as British actors often play havoc with transatlantic accents), rarely acknowledging the existence of any 'British accent' other than Scots or Cockney.

Fortunately, Heston's care with his preparation paid off and he achieved an accurate reproduction of the speech patterns of a man of Gordon's nationality, background and status. The achievement did not come cheaply. He spent many weeks with a speech teacher, nightly taping long passages for practice. He commented upon his near-obsession with such matters in an interview for the London *Evening Standard*, explaining that he felt that if he got 'everything right about the part and [did] everything in the right way it all helps to make the performance look good'.

After thousands of British soldiers are massacred by the fanatical followers of the Mahdi (Laurence Olivier), the British government hear

Riding out into the desert on his way to meet the Mahdi in Khartoum.

a report on the situation brought to them by Colonel J. D. H. Stewart (Richard Johnson). From this it is clear that the Mahdi is engaged in a holy war which will end only when all foreigners are driven from Egypt; his main target is Khartoum, in the Sudan, from which city the British control Suez. The Prime Minister, William Gladstone (Ralph Richardson), is aware that an attempt must be made to prevent another massacre, but he knows that the British army is at full stretch. Astutely, but with extreme cynicism, Gladstone decides that he will not send troops – just General Gordon. The General is expected to use his considerable reputation to hold Khartoum against the Mahdi. If he fails it will be his personal failure and not the fault of the government. When the proposal is made to Gordon he accepts, even though the Prime Minister's duplicity is apparent to him.

When Gordon reaches Egypt he quickly learns that the Mahdi has captured the minds and allegiance of many who were once pro-British.

Nevertheless, there is a favourable response to Gordon. Encouraged by this, and despite the fact that supplies are low and the Mahdi's men are everywhere causing unrest, he determines to meet the man he must defeat. He goes into the desert with only one companion as guide and meets with the Mahdi. Gordon offers to withdraw the Egyptian army in return for the Mahdi's agreement not to persist with his attacks upon his fellow countrymen. The Mahdi refuses. With single-minded fanaticism he declares his determination to carry out the will of Mohammed and take Khartoum 'in blood'.

Returning to Khartoum, the General prepares to defend the city as best he can. An attempt to send some civilians to safety comes to a disastrous end when their ship is intercepted and they are killed, proof being supplied by the Mahdi in the form of severed heads and the hand of Colonel Stewart, who was in charge of the escape attempt. The Mahdi, who shows a wary respect for his opponent's own strength of mind in *his* beliefs, offers Gordon a chance to leave. The General refuses, opting instead to stay and fight the hopeless battle for Khartoum.

The city is attacked, its inhabitants massacred and Gordon meets his end when a spear is driven through his chest. As his head is hoisted on high for all to see, the city is razed. But all this death and destruction leads to plague; soon the numbers of the Mahdi's followers are dramatically diminished and the Mahdi too succumbs.

Looking the part of General Charles 'China' Gordon for Khartoum.

His suspicion of the British government is shared by Richard Johnson and Alexander Knox in Khartoum.

The film measured up well to its potential although proving nowhere nearly as commercially successful as might have been hoped. The spectacle is as compelling as would be expected with Yakima Canutt as second unit director. The personal conflicts and political chicanery are well captured and fine acting performances abound. Olivier's Mahdi carries with it faint foreshadowings of his Othello, while Richardson's Gladstone is a triumph of shifty-eyed deviousness.

In the central role Heston does extremely well with perhaps the most complex character he has ever played. Gordon was a strange man, part soldier, part mystic, who exuded a fanaticism and belief in the rightness of all that he did which matched that of the Mahdi. Assured and dedicated, he must have known he was accepting a death warrant from the moment he first met Gladstone, but he strode towards his fate with a stoic disregard for his own safety that makes any storybook character pale into insignificance. In Gordon can be seen all the characteristics that represented the best and worst of imperial Britain. It is to Heston's credit that he brings out all the nuances in the character of this man whose background, so far removed from Heston's own, must have been hard for him to imagine. Yet Gordon's responses to the world in which he made so great a mark, especially his arrogant defiance to the point of martyrdom, closely resemble those of many of the other characters Heston has chosen to play.

In 1985, the year of the centenary of Gordon's death, Heston was invited to the National Gallery in London for the occasion of the restoration to public view of G. W. Joy's famous painting of the General's death, which had long lain unseen in the basement of the Leeds Art Gallery.

In ironic contrast to this, an article that appeared in the same year in *The London Hotel Magazine* on the subject of Madame Tussaud's waxwork museum was accompanied by a photograph showing Charlton Heston's head (in the guise of Gordon) consigned to oblivion at Wookey Hole in Somerset, where row upon row of redundant wax heads and other appendages are stored. Next to the Heston/Gordon head lay, to the right, the head of William Gladstone (the real one, not Ralph Richardson), while to the left lay the feet of Elizabeth Taylor.

Almost any film which followed *Khartoum* would have been anticlimactic, but *Counterpoint* (1967) barely makes the attempt to rise to the occasion. Based on Alan Sillitoe's novel *The General*, the story concerns the conductor of a symphony orchestra, Lionel Evans (Heston), who is performing in Europe during World War II. Caught up in the broader conflict, Evans also locks horns with a Nazi officer, General Schiller (Maximilian Schell), who wants the orchestra to perform for his men. Evans refuses, even though the musicians are less concerned with the morality of their situation than with staying alive. Eventually, Evans is forced to concede that theirs is the approach to adopt. Finally, as the Germans plan to execute the orchestra, Evans joins his men when they decide to fight. The majority of the musicians escape but Evans is captured by Colonel Arndt (Anton Diffring). The Colonel is about to shoot Evans but is himself killed by Schiller.

Although well acted throughout, the film does not grip as it should even though the central premise, that of the responses of artists caught up in war, is potentially interesting. The long essays in moral philosophy engaged in by the conductor and the German commander lie at the core of the problem, despite strong performances from the two principals, especially Schell. The resulting whole is a shade too *largo* for the enjoyment of most filmgoers, who generally prefer their war movies to be at least *vivace*.

For this role, Heston added the skills of the orchestral conductor – or at least the simulation of such skills – to the long list of accomplishments he had acquired for his film roles. In the more harassed moments of his portrayal he conveys something of the tetchiness of a Leonard Bernstein, but he seems to lack the emotional depths of, say, a Solti. In

Scrapping with Gene Rutherford in Will Penny *while Bruce Dern prepares to weigh in.*

the non-musical passages of *Counterpoint*, however, Heston's portrayal does not carry enough conviction, which helps Schell's German commander win most of their scenes together.

Heston had first read the novel on which his next film was based during an aeroplane flight in August 1966. As he indicates in his *Journals*, he was so impressed that he even overcame the caution he felt when he learned that the author was prepared to sell his book only if he could direct the film. Despite his wariness at working with a man who had only limited previous experience working in TV, Heston agreed. In the event, it proved to be a wise decision to accept *Will Penny* (1967), however unlikely it might have seemed as a vehicle for the man who had played Moses, Ben-Hur and 'China' Gordon.

Will Penny (Heston) is an illiterate cowpuncher who, fast approaching the age of fifty, knows that his years in the saddle are numbered and all that awaits him is a bleak and lonely future. Signing off after a long, hard cattle drive, Will rides away with two friends, Blue and Dutchy (Lee Majors and Anthony Zerbe), in search of work to see them through the winter. After camping overnight by a river, Blue and

The epitome of the faded, illiterate, drifting cowboy in Will Penny.

Beans again? Questioning the quality of the chow in Will Penny.

Dutchy spot an elk, but as they prepare to shoot it the animal falls to someone else's gunfire. Across the river are silhouetted the menacing figures of Preacher Quint (Donald Pleasence) and his unappetizing family. Reluctantly, Blue and Dutchy back away from their first chance of fresh meat in a long time but one of the Quints starts shooting and soon Will, who until now has been sleeping, is forced to help his friends; it is his shot which kills one of Quint's three sons. Threatening to catch up and get even, the Preacher backs off.

Dutchy has also been hurt, and his companions take him in search of a doctor, along the way pausing to eat and drink at a staging post where Catherine Allen (Joan Hackett) is resting on her journey to California to join her husband. After putting Dutchy in the care of Doctor Fraker (William Schallert), Blue elects to stay in town while Will goes in search of work. He finds a dead cowboy and takes the body to the Flatiron ranch. There he is hired as the dead man's replacement by foreman Alex (Ben Johnson), although the other cowpokes are mistrustful of the newcomer; they believe that he might be responsible for creating the job vacancy he has just filled. Alex sends Will off to ride the line, which means he will be gone the whole of the winter. At the line-rider's cabin he finds Catherine and her son Horace (Jon Francis), who have been deserted by their guide. He rides off, telling her to be gone when he returns.

But Will has been spotted by the vengeful Quint family, who bide their time before wounding him and leaving him half-naked in the snow. He manages to make it back to the cabin, where he is cared for by Catherine. An attachment develops between the two adults, and also between Will and young Horace. It is Christmas and as they prepare for a celebration of sorts, the Quints arrive. Will is tied up and mauled inquisitively by Quint's daughter while his two surviving sons fight over Catherine like dogs scrapping over a bone. Later while Will slaves away for the Quints, Catherine contrives to set the two sons against one another. Will takes advantage of this diversion and makes a run for it. Then Blue and Dutchy arrive in search of their friend, and together the three men devise a plan to smoke the Quints out of the cabin by pouring a bag of sulphur down the chimney.

The Quints are wiped out as Alex and the rest of the cowboys from the ranch ride up, having been alerted to possible trouble by the fact that Flatiron cattle are roaming freely all over the range.

Will quits his job and, despite Catherine's plea that he should make a life with her and Horace, he rides off with Blue and Dutchy. He knows that the odds are against Catherine's suggestion working out and rather than risk bringing unhappiness to her and the boy he consciously abandons forever any hope of a life that will be anything other than empty and unhappy.

Altogether different from the usual run of western movie, *Will Penny* is a bleakly realistic account of the hard and constricted life open to men like Will, who lived the real lives on which Hollywood based so many fanciful, overly glamorized accounts. Despite Heston's early misgivings, Tom Gries's direction is very capable and his is a closely observed and finely drawn study of the everyday humdrum yet thoroughly fascinating reality of the cowboy's life. The unglamorous side of the small towns through which these men ride is depicted every bit as well as in Sam Peckinpah's mining-camp sequence in *Guns in the Afternoon*.

All the supporting roles are played with dour and believable sincerity. Joan Hackett's Catherine, inarticulately shy but growing in confidence as she realizes that in Will she has met someone even less equipped than she to face the harsh world, is excellent. Anthony Zerbe and Ben Johnson turn in the kind of high-grade performances of which they have proved consistently capable. Even Lee Majors, whose TV roles have tended to submerge him in technology and who usually fails to make a mark on the big screen, rises to the occasion. Donald

105

Pleasence is repellently convincing in his justifiably over-the-top portrayal of the crazy Quint. Lydia Heston plays the role of Mrs Fraker, the doctor's wife.

It is, however, Heston's performance which holds the attention. On screen almost without pause, he becomes the epitome of the faded cowboy, showing uncertainty and vulnerability, two characteristics he had rarely if ever been called upon to display before. That he could do so at all was surely an answer to those critics who considered him incapable of such a performance. That he does it in such a compelling and deeply moving manner should have buried such criticism for ever.

Unfortunately, seemingly unaware of what they had, the studio allowed *Will Penny* to slip into release without fuss and as a result it was to be many years before the film's true worth became apparent. Seen again, almost two decades on, this performance and the film itself stand as major achievements both in the career of the star and in the long and wide-ranging canon of the Hollywood western.

There was another factor which helped *Will Penny* slip by unnoticed on its release. This was the tremendous fuss and excitement which surrounded another Heston film, his first foray into the world of science fiction.

Planet of the Apes (1968), based upon a story by Pierre Boulle, benefited from a first-draft screenplay by Rod Serling, whose numerous credits had illuminated TV's 'Playhouse 90' and who also created and wrote the bulk of the cult science-fiction series *Twilight Zone*. Later, Michael Wilson substantially changed Serling's original work. The idea was decidedly cinematic, but even so it was a long time before producer Arthur Jacobs could raise financial backing. Once he did, from Twentieth Century-Fox, the film went ahead with great speed and considerably secrecy. For once, a studio recognized a good idea before it was laid in front of them.

George Taylor (Heston) is commander of an interplanetary space flight leaving Earth on a mission which will take the equivalent of 2,000 years in real time. He and his crew members go into suspended animation; when they awaken the spacecraft is out of control and about to crash-land on to a strange planet. Taylor and two others who survive the crash soon find themselves in an environment much like Earth's, inhabited by savage quasi-human creatures who are being hunted by intelligent, horse-riding, gun-carrying apes who can also speak a language he understands. He cannot respond to them, however,

Just one of the many problems of working with animals – as Heston and Linda Harrison discovered in Planet of the Apes.

Making a last stand for mankind, to the discomfort of Maurice Evans in Planet of the Apes.

because in a fight he has been shot in the throat. After being taken prisoner, he is endlessly interrogated but cannot speak. Eventually the apes, who fear the fact that he is clearly more intelligent than the other human types on the planet, decide that he shall be lobotomized and castrated. Overhearing this, Taylor escapes and hides in a museum which contains many objects he half recognizes – and one which he fully identifies: the stuffed and mounted body of one of his crewmen. Then he is recaptured, but his throat wound has now healed sufficiently for him to speak; the apes are shaken to realize that this creature, whom they regard as an animal, can communicate with them.

The apes' leader, Dr Zaius (Maurice Evans), decides that Taylor must be tried in order to determine whether he is a threat to the ordered society of the apes. If he is, then he will die. Taylor has no doubt that the trial will be rigged, for if he were to win the planet's society would collapse. Bound and gagged, he is unable to speak in his own defence and is found guilty, but two of the apes have grown to like him. They are Zira and Cornelius (Kim Stanley and Roddy McDowall). After helping him to escape, these two, with another ape, Lucius (Lou Wagner), and a female human, Nova (Linda Harrison), ride away with Taylor into the Forbidden Zone. There they come upon something which Taylor recognizes. It is a part of a house, exactly like those back on Earth. Slowly, Taylor begins to realize that at some time in the past this must have been a planet like Earth on which human beings were the masters, but with the passage of time they have been superseded by the apes. Later, as they ride along the coast, Taylor sees something protruding from the sand and he finally accepts the truth of what has only been hinted at thus far.

What he sees are the remnants of the Statue of Liberty. This is not a planet *like* Earth; this *is* Earth at some time in the future from when he left it.

Despite some uncertainties in script and plotting, *Planet of the Apes* deserved its success. The essential implausibility of its central plot is overcome by thoughtful casting and make-up for the ape characters. By using skilled actors where many film-makers would have settled for hiding nobodies beneath the plastic faces, the apes have strength and credibility. McDowall and Stanley both avoid the trap of falling into parody, as does Maurice Evans. As the only human character with a major role, Heston was more animated than in almost any other film he had made up to this point in his career. Ceaselessly on the run or undergoing torment and ridicule at the hands of the apes, he was obliged to draw upon many levels of ability he had previously only tapped lightly, if at all. As different as could be from Will Penny, his George Taylor proved a memorable role, but not for any qualities of his acting. Rather it was the unusual nature of the film which stayed in the mind. Given that his was the only major non-ape role in the movie, it is not surprising that Heston does well, although the old adage that actors should never work with animals must surely be doubly potent when those animals can speak. The part undoubtedly called for more action than acting, but those scenes in which Taylor is rendered temporarily inarticulate convey the character's frustrated fears so well that they help lift the movie in a manner entirely necessary if the film was to be anything other than just another sci-fi romp.

Heston was just as active and as subject to brutality in his next film role, although this time the individuals dishing out the punishment were fellow human beings.

Number One (1968) traces the last few weeks in the playing career of Ron 'Cat' Catlan (Heston) who, at 40, has reached, if not actually passed, the point where he should quit. But if he does retire what is there left for him? A friend, former football player Richie Fowler (Bruce Dern), tries to persuade him to join his car-leasing business, but Cat is determined to soldier on. With his wife Julie (Jessica Walter) intent

Heston's most physically demanding role, in Number One.

only on running her dress-designing business, he takes some solace in the company of Ann Marley (Diana Muldaur), but even this relationship proves to be no substitute for the game.

Battered, bruised and despite having undergone surgery on one knee, Cat hangs on despite the attempts of a younger man to replace him in the team, the New Orleans Saints. His affair with Ann over, Cat takes to the field watched by his wife and Richie. There he is booed by the crowd, who now hate the man they formerly idolized for having failed to retain the heroic quality with which they themselves have imbued him. Nevertheless, he hopes to recover his standing and retain his place on the team. He plays well and helps his side towards a major victory, but then he is caught and tackled by two giants from the opposing team who leave him, an ignominious and broken figure, lying on the turf of the arena.

Heston trained hard for and performed well in this role, drawing praise even from the real New Orleans Saints who worked on the film with him. Craig Fertig, the experienced coach who helped train him, was also favourably impressed – although, as Heston comments in his *Journals*, he was careful with his use of praise. 'I think,' Fertig remarked to the film's producer, 'he's getting to the point where he has delusions of adequacy.'

Claiming it to be the most physically demanding role of his career, Heston rightly thought highly of this film, which, like *Will Penny*, was directed by Tom Gries. American audiences were more reserved. The time for this type of story, which exposed the harsh world of top-level sports, especially from the viewpoint of ageing stars, was still a few years ahead; it would later be treated with similar openness in such films as *North Dallas 40* (also about football) and *Slap Shot* (about ice hockey). British audiences had no chance to see *Number One* for themselves: it was never shown, because at this time American football had yet to make its impact on the sporting scene in Britain.

Overall, this was another case of a good film being allowed to slip away by faithless and unimaginative distributors. Even latterday TV audiences in America rarely have a chance to see it, despite the fact that its quality places it at least on a par with its successors.

It was especially unfortunate for Heston that this film was allowed to disappear, for Catlan was among his best roles and Heston rises admirably to the opportunity of stretching himself in one of the few non-uniformed twentieth-century roles of his career. It was also a rare opportunity for him to play an out-and-out loser, yet he does so with commendable sensitivity. In failing at the only thing in life at which he might have stood a chance of success, Ron Catlan mirrors a million fears and frustrations; Heston conveys all this without self-pity or loss of dignity. It is a fine performance in a film which, if re-released, would very probably find today a more discerning audience on both sides of the Atlantic.

As the 1960s came towards their close, Heston could look back on a highly successful decade of film-making during which he had made movies that were successful with the critics and with the public, although not necessarily scoring on both counts at the same time. He had made epic films of high quality in *El Cid* and *Khartoum*; he had made others that missed being great through post-production interference or lack of promotion – *Major Dundee*, *The War Lord* and *Number One*; he had achieved enormous box-office popularity with *Planet of the Apes*; and he had made one film, *Will Penny*, which revealed a substantially greater range in him as an actor, even if it was to lie dormant for several years before a far wider audience could see it, thanks to television, and thus enjoy the best role of his career.

Most importantly, the misjudgement he had displayed in choosing roles, up to and possibly including that of Michelangelo, was at last under control. Of his last six film roles only that of the orchestral conductor, for which he had learned yet another skill during his pre-production build-up, might be considered a flawed selection. Such a high ratio of winners proved too good to last.

Off the screen he was deeply involved in many activities, not least his work with SAG, his private life with his family and his obsession with tennis. There had also been whispers of a political career. Past presidents of SAG had included George Murphy and Ronald Reagan, both of whom had gone on to important political posts, Murphy as majority Senator for California and Reagan as State Governor before reaching for and attaining the White House. In later years, Heston's successor as president of the Guild, the actor John Gavin, continued to demonstrate the value of the post as a jumping-off point for a political career by becoming US Ambassador to Mexico. Heston, however, declared himself to be uninterested in such a career.

This did not mean that he had no political views: quite the contrary, in fact, for he was always ready to talk politics during interviews. In one, for the London *Evening Standard*, he expounded upon a topic which has frustrated many of those Americans who take a logical view of politics without giving due consideration to the rules by which the game is traditionally played. 'We get into terrible trouble,' he said, speaking of the USA, 'because we undertake an idealistic solution to problems other countries prefer to ignore.'

For now, however, he had too many film projects with which to occupy his mind and time. Not least of these was his determination to return to something he had not touched on film since his amateur performance for David Bradley – the work of William Shakespeare.

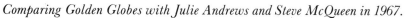

Comparing Golden Globes with Julie Andrews and Steve McQueen in 1967.

C H A P T E R
Six

'. . . the absolutely indispensable creative
presence is the director.'
Charlton Heston

Since his early days at drama school Heston has maintained an abiding passion for the works of William Shakespeare. He believed then, and still believes, that an actor must play in the great classical dramas if his career is to have any meaning. Yet he has always been equally aware that if an American actor has ambitions to play Shakespeare, in whatever medium, he will have an uphill struggle against indifference if not outright hostility.

He had, of course, acted in Shakespeare in the theatre and on TV, but apart from his performance as Antony in *Julius Caesar* for David Bradley he had not so far been able to play a Shakespearean role on film. Now, as a mature and accomplished actor, he clearly hankered after bringing his big-screen talents to bear on the Bard.

Of course, he was far from being the first. The film industries of America and Britain had ventured Shakespeare movies of variable quality since the earliest days, when the aim, in the main, was little more than to film theatrical productions. Back in the silent era, such movies had an understandably limited appeal, but even after the advent of the talkies box-office response to Shakespeare was generally poor. As a result, the major studios tended to view the Bard with a wary eye and before World War II big-budget productions were decidedly few and far between. An exception was Warner Brothers' *A Midsummer Night's Dream* (1935) with James Cagney, Mickey Rooney, Olivia de Havilland and Dick Powell heading a long string of contract players. The result was a remarkably creditable effort, but the box-office was still less than what it would have been had the same team and effort been put into a routine programmer.

113

After World War II the situation changed following the great critical and commercial success of Laurence Olivier's *Henry V* (1945), which effectively caught the upturned spirits of Britain at the time. Olivier's *Hamlet* followed three years later and others came in its wake, although both Hollywood and British film-makers were often content merely to take the storylines and reset them in updated locales. *Joe Macbeth* (1955) was a fair example (made in Britain with American money and stars) and even better was *All Night Long* (1962), which transposed *Othello* into a story of jazz musicians in contemporary London with great flair, aided in considerable part by Patrick McGoohan's convincingly conniving, jazz-drumming Iago.

Flair and imagination were rarely present together, however, and when they were, as in Akira Kurosawa's transposed version of *Macbeth*, *Throne of Blood* (1957), or Orson Welles' *Chimes at Midnight* (1966), critical acclaim was not matched by support from the paying customers.

Not surprisingly, given their commercial orientation, the major studios with their big budgets and stars preferred to stay in the wings, although the 1953 version of *Julius Caesar* proved that audiences *would* go and see Shakespeare if someone with the popular appeal of Marlon Brando held centre screen.

Perhaps the only constant factors with major Shakespearean films are that those which have stayed stuffily close to the theatrical concept have done badly at the box-office, while those that took substantial liberties with the original text, though guaranteed a critical hammering, at least stood a chance of recouping the cost of the negative. Only rarely, as with *Henry V*, did a film's makers succeed in striking the right balance. The fact that the film industry, on both sides of the Atlantic, had set few precedents for verisimilitude and was open to concepts which broadened out the original play suited Heston when he prepared to make his professional film début in Shakespeare.

Heston had no desire to run riot through the original texts – quite the contrary, in fact – but he certainly felt no compulsion to approach Shakespeare with undue reverence. He had no time for those who felt that every word was sacrosanct, remarking in his *Journals* that he would bet his soul that even Shakespeare would have cut and adapted his own work in his own time. Like many actors, Heston requires room for manoeuvre with his lines, not merely in interpretation but by way of change either after deliberation or by instinctive improvisation. Such behaviour, while eminently reasonable, disturbs some writers of plays and motion-picture scripts who are unshakable in their belief that for an actor to change one word, even an inflection, is akin to scrawling on

'O mighty Caesar! Dost thou lie so low?' As Mark Antony in Julius Caesar.

the Tablets of Moses with a felt-tip pen. While showing due regard for
quality material, Heston has never been afraid to redact to suit the
purposes of the medium or the needs of the production.

In deciding to make a motion picture based upon a Shakespeare
play, he was conscious of that uncertain ground he was treading. He
knew all about the many precedents, their limited commercial success
and the fact that most had suffered a severe drubbing at the hands of
the critics, who have never fully come to terms with the desire of some
film-makers to perform works from classical theatre in the upstart

115

medium. That *American* actors should have the temerity to wish to perform Shakespearean roles is also a guarantee that some British critics will work themselves up into near-apoplectic rage.

In choosing *Julius Caesar* (1970), Heston was wisely displaying an element of caution. There had been half a dozen previous screen versions of the play, the most recent being that with Brando as Antony, the role Heston had chosen. The attraction of the play to contemporary performers and audiences undoubtedly lies in its political machinations, especially the self-serving plot of his closest associates to assassinate Caesar and the subsequent justifications and recriminations among the plotters. Although John Kennedy's assassination had occurred seven years before, the event was still sufficiently fresh in most minds for the play to carry certain echoes (not entirely justified, except in the minds of those who either held to the conspiracy theory or were unsure about the alternatives).

In the event this version, in the production of which Heston was undoubtedly the driving force, worked well enough on most levels even if, by opening up the tight confines of the original and offering battle scenes, some additions were made which were essential neither to the plot nor to the motivation of the characters.

Alarmed at the apparent ambitions of Julius Caesar (John Gielgud), his political colleagues, urged on by the devious Cassius (Richard Johnson), decide to kill him. Only Brutus (Jason Robards) hesitates, agonizing over the moral dilemma with which he is faced. Aware that Mark Antony (Heston), who is Caesar's friend, will oppose them, the conspirators hatch the assassination plot in his absence. After Caesar's death, Antony is allowed to speak at the funeral, and his subtly constructed oration not only turns his fellow Romans against the conspirators but brings about a further revolution within the Senate, which brings Octavius (Richard Chamberlain) to a position of power. This action has major ramifications for the future, for Octavius's apparent weaknesses will prove detrimental to the continued authority of Rome.

The bulk of the cast was drawn from the British stage. Gielgud is a suitably equivocal Caesar, while Richard Johnson's Cassius is perhaps the best performance in the film, bringing to his important role, which carries so much of the story's substrata, great depths of personal commitment and political machination. Heston's Antony is always sound but at times suffers mildly from a measure of diffidence in performance. Nevertheless, there are moments when he attains a high level of conviction, especially in the funeral oration. Although he stays closer to the traditional interpretation of the text, he does not prove to be quite as memorable as Brando's brooding if mannered presence in the 1953 version. The major flaw of the film, apart from stodgy direction from Stuart Burge, lies in Jason Robards' playing of the key role of Brutus. As the moral dilemma of the play centres upon Brutus and his gradual swing from a natural reluctance to commit a grievous act against Caesar to his decision to join the conspirators, the part needs to be played with the utmost power and conviction. Although a gifted actor with many very fine performances to his credit both before and after this, Robards fails utterly to come to grips with the nuances of the character. From the harsh comments he confided to his *Journals*, it is clear that Heston was fully aware of his fellow actor's shortcomings in the role long before it eventually reached the screen.

In the event, with the core of the film irretrievably weakened, the critical and popular response was poor. Even so, Heston was determined to take another shot at Shakespeare on film – once again in the role of Antony, but in a different play. The next time he would also ensure that the film was much more under his personal control. But before that he had other films to make, this time aimed at the more commercially acceptable end of the moviemakers' spectrum; these would give him the opportunity to earn the money he needed before he could bring Shakespeare to the screen again.

Before making *Julius Caesar* Heston had fulfilled an agreement he had reached with the producer of *Planet of the Apes* to make an appearance in the planned sequel. In *Beneath the Planet of the Apes* (1969) he again takes the role of astronaut George Taylor, who has returned to Earth 2,000 years hence. On this occasion the leading role is taken by James Franciscus as another astronaut, Brent, sent out to discover what has become of the first expedition. Once again intellectually advanced apes are fighting a human sub-species, this time a group with telepathic powers who crazily worship a primed Doomsday weapon. Eventually, realizing that with Taylor and the human telepaths all dead, he is the only human left on Earth, Brent unleashes this super-bomb in order to destroy the world.

Brent's decision, which essentially asserts that no world at all is better than a world without mankind, says much for the film's makers' feeling of self-importance. The assertion is not supported by their product. Although the series would continue with considerable commercial success this second swing at the concept is really rather poor.

Heston's role is essentially a cameo, although the scenes he made during the few days he spent working on the film are structured to give the appearance of his playing an important part in the progression of the story. His performance is best described as perfunctory. During the making of this film he had been more interested in his preparations for *Julius Caesar* – and it shows.

In *The Hawaiians* (1970) (originally released in Britain as *The Master of the Islands*), Heston plays the role of Whip Hoxworth, a generally unpleasant individual working in late nineteenth-century Hawaii. When his grandfather dies leaving the bulk of his estate to Micah (Alec McCowen), a relative he already dislikes, Hoxworth heads for a patch of land he has inherited taking with him his wife Purity (Geraldine Chaplin) and a couple of the numerous Chinese labourers he has shipped over from the mainland. The Chinese are Nuyk Tsin (Tina Chen) and her husband Mun Ki (Mako), and the four of them slowly turn the barren soil into a plantation on which they grow a plant new to the islands, the pineapple. Eventually, Purity leaves her husband in order to raise their son Noel (John Philip Law) in the traditional ways of Hawaii. The Chinese couple also depart when Mun Ki contracts leprosy, but they leave their five children in Hoxworth's care.

With the passage of time the plantation owner, who has taken a Japanese girl, Fumiko (Miko Mayama), as his mistress, changes, becoming a responsible citizen determined to bring status and wealth to the Islands. He assists in overthrowing the royal ruler of the Islands and replacing her with the nation's first president, Micah, with whom he is now reconciled. After fighting off plague, during which the previously wealthy Nuyk Tsin is ruined, Hoxworth sees his son Noel marry Nuyk Tsin's daughter and a new dynasty is born.

The storyline of the film, which derives from a small section towards the end of James A. Michener's sprawling novel *Hawaii*, is confused and rambling and neither screenplay nor direction are very secure. The main performers, among whom Tina Chen and Mako are especially effective, generally deserved better support. Heston's commanding presence gave the impression that he really could have helped put Hawaii on the map, but the dialogue he is obliged to speak fails to measure up to the visual image. Part of the responsibility lies in the fact that in the novel the character he plays is largely subordinate to Nuyk Tsin; indeed, Heston has indicated his awareness that in the restructuring of the narrative to justify his top billing much coherence was lost.

Heston's prestige had, by now, extended far beyond such matters as where his name appeared on movie posters. Indeed, it was sufficient to attract politicians. But his life was a full one: his off-screen activities continued apace, and every moment of his time, when he was neither filming nor preparing to film, nor playing tennis, was fully occupied. Towards the end of 1969 he was approached by a group of Democrats who asked him to run for the United States Senate. He considered the idea, and, no doubt, what he would have to sacrifice in order to undertake a political career, but Lydia was against it and ultimately he refused, indicating in his *Journals* that, however trivial it might sound, he really wanted to act.

Later, in 1971, he ended his sixth successive term as president of SAG, in which he was succeeded by John Gavin at the first contested election for the post. Shortly before handing over, Heston led a deputation to the White House to plead the Hollywood case for special consideration for tax concessions which would allow more money to be ploughed back into film-making. President Nixon was unable to offer much hope but Heston reported that they had been given a warm and sympathetic hearing. In 1972 he again acknowledged his approval of the President, hailing him for his demonstrations of deep concern for American cultural life by providing the leadership that was essential if the arts were to receive increased funding. Politically, Heston also found himself supporting the President through activities with the Democrats for Nixon lobby, although this may have been as much in opposition to George McGovern as it was in support of the incumbent.

As movie stars' obsessions go, tennis must be one of the most harmless and least fattening.

Also at this time Heston had become interested in the activities of the American Film Institute. Until now, however, his commitment to the Screen Actors' Guild had prevented him from becoming involved. Once he had relinquished the office he held with SAG, he was able to take part in the work of the AFI. Before long he was appointed Chairman.

For his next film role Heston was once more involved in a bleak science-fiction view of the future. This was *The Omega Man* (1971), the second film to be based upon Richard Matheson's novel *I Am Legend*.

Robert Neville (Heston) lives in Los Angeles were he believes himself to be the only normal human being left on Earth after biological warfare has destroyed most of human life. Neville, a scientist, has been working on an antidote, but has discovered the answer too late to save mankind. The only other survivors he knows of are some mutants who have become albinos and cannot withstand any direct light. Led by Matthias (Anthony Zerbe), they can only leave their subterranean ghetto at night. Matthias, once a famed TV pundit, seeks Neville's death in atonement for the catastrophe. Under his leadership the mutants spend their nights trying to invade Neville's apartment, in which he keeps supplies of food regularly supplemented by trips to the broken and plundered supermarkets. To discourage the mutants, Neville has encircled his home with generator-driven lights.

While on an expedition to renew his clothing at a store in the once-great city, Neville realizes that another normal human being, a girl, is here, but she vanishes before he can speak to her. Later, he is captured by Matthias's mutant horde, but as they prepare to burn him at the stake in the middle of the Los Angeles Coliseum, the floodlights are turned on. As the mutants rush from the light Neville is freed by the girl and a companion. The girl's name is Lisa (Rosaline Cash). She is one of a small group who have survived but are slowly falling victim to the plague. Neville helps them, using his own blood as a makeshift antidote, but then decides to return to his apartment for the serum. The girl, who is black, goes with him and, after fighting off another attack by the mutants, Neville and Lisa make love.

The next day, as they prepare to leave the city for the last time, Lisa is stricken with the sickness. He rescues her from the mutants but is mortally wounded. Lisa's friends arrive, find the serum in Neville's pockets and are thus able to ensure the survival of the human race.

Much of the film is very good, especially the scenes of Heston alone in the empty city. Much credit for this goes to the photographer, Russell Metty, with whom Heston was working again. Also interesting are most of the special effects. On the debit side are the scenes with the mutants, most of which appear to be staged as a deliberate parody of a vampire movie. Even if the intention were acceptable, the manner of execution of these scenes is not, and neither are the occasional and ultimately successful attempts to martyr Neville. For this much of the blame lies with unimaginative staging by director Boris Sagal, who had a much more successful later career as a director in TV.

Performances are uneven: Anthony Zerbe is believable as he always is, and Rosalind Cash gives a good performance despite the doubtful, quasi-hipsterish dialogue she is required to speak. The other roles are all fortunately minor, but with better dialogue all could have been improved upon. Heston's performance is variable. When he is alone and holding conversations with himself, or with the decaying corpses that confront him at every turn, or conversing with the bust of Caesar which sits across the table from him when he plays chess, he is very good indeed. He is also effective in the action-man sequences. In the more intimate confrontations with Rosalind Cash he is less convincing, once again displaying his reluctance to be open in his on-screen personal relationships.

Although not an emotionally intense film, it is this persistent failing of Heston's which most weakens the story. Even at its most basic level, the man-woman relationship between these two characters should have greater fire. Admittedly, Lisa knows a handful of other men, but Neville believes himself to be alone on the planet save for the mutants. The level of interest he displays towards this highly attractive young woman who suddenly enters his life is remarkably subdued. Simple, unadorned lust would have been better than the restraint he demonstrates.

Heston's performance in *Call of the Wild* (1972) is one which few people have been able to see, for the film received only limited European screenings and no cinema release in the United States. Based on Jack London's splendid tale, the film traces the adventures of a German shepherd dog named Buck. While living a comfortable Californian existence it is stolen and taken to Alaska, where it is sold to John Thornton (Heston), who wants to use the animal on the mail run between Skagway and Dawson City. After quarrelling with Black Burton (George Eastman) over the very obvious charms of saloon-keeper Calliope Laurent (Michèle Mercier), Thornton finds Buck has been stolen, along with the rest of the dog team. Stranded, John and his companion Pete (Raimund Harmstorf) pursue the thieves, who eventually die of exposure. Thornton assists Calliope in building a hotel but cannot make her break with Burton, whose help she also needs.

Listening for the Call of the Wild, *a deservedly obscure film.*

Thornton and Pete answer to the lure of gold while Buck answers the call of the wild and mates with a wolf. Eventually Thornton and Pete strike it rich when they find a legendary gold mine. But this is Indian holy ground and when Indians discover them the two prospectors are killed. Buck attacks the Indians, killing those who have killed his master. The dog now runs off to join the wolves becoming, in his turn, an Indian legend.

This film lacks the strong, unsentimental narrative drive of the original Jack London story. An international co-production, with Britain, Germany, Spain, Italy and France getting into the act, it suffers from many of the problems such ventures frequently encounter. In this instance, despite well-photographed locations (in Norway), there is a muddled script and meandering and frequently imprecise direction from Ken Annakin.

The acting is variable, as also often happens when half the actors are called upon to speak in a language they understand only dimly, if at all. Mouthing lines which are due to be overdubbed is no way to achieve projection of those nuances of character which are needed if a film is to be anything more than mediocre. Given the problems with which he is surrounded, Heston's performance is adequate but is one he perhaps wishes he had not undertaken, at least not in such unsatisfactory circumstances.

Although much of Jack London's writing can be read simply in terms of adventure yarns of the great outdoors, and his characters can be seen as uncomplicated men of action, there is always much greater depth for the perceptive reader. When his tales have been transformed into movies the adventure elements are always preserved but rarely are the depths explored. Given *Call of the Wild*'s multi-national problems it was too much to expect anything other than the customary skim-over-the-surface. This is especially unfortunate for Heston, who undoubtedly had the ability to make more of this particular story. Indeed, as some of his later films reflect, he has a genuine interest in the regions wherein London set many of his adventures, but he does not make a strong enough impact in this film to lift it from its deserved obscurity.

Although he had long resisted calls to direct a film, Heston finally acceded in order to bring to his next Shakespearean role all the ideas he had been developing over the years.

His view of the status of the director is unequivocal. 'I feel very strongly that the director is supposed to be the boss. Art was never created by democracy,' he once observed. Elaborating upon this theme, he further underlined his respect for the director's role at the expense of the screenwriter's, possibly as a result of having had to work with less than professional efforts over the years, but also subordinating his own status as an actor. 'Cinema is a director's medium. It is written even less than it is acted, but it is primarily the director's medium. There are films for which actors are required, although this is not true of all roles, by any means . . . but the absolutely indispensable creative presence is the director.'

Apart from his acting talent and his as yet untried ability as a director, the Shakespeare play he wanted to make was backed by his own money, and thus became a highly personal film both in concept and in execution.

Antony and Cleopatra (1972) takes up the story of Mark Antony some years after the death of Julius Caesar, tracing the decline of a once-proud man now brought low by his all-consuming love for a predatory woman who has no conception of moral values.

In his writings and in interviews, Heston has made much of the essentially cinematic qualities of this particular play of Shakespeare's, and for the most part he succeeds admirably in realizing them. He was well aware of the criticism he was inviting. 'I know,' he remarked in a *New York Times* interview, 'people will say "Oh God, he's doing Antony with the gladiators." But I submit that I am doing it in cinematic terms.' He went on to suggest that the play was in a sense too big for the theatre: given that this is one of the least performed of Shakespeare's plays, he may well be right.

The adverse advance critical reaction was followed by more of the same when the critics had a chance to see the finished film, but subsequent viewings suggest that once again the critics were unable to overcome their own limited view of how things should be done; their reactions seem to intimate yet again that Shakespeare really should not be filmed at all, but, if it must be, then it certainly should not be done by Americans.

In fact, the film has many fine qualities in its structure, which owes much to Heston's interpretation of the play and his directorial control. The often startling rejigging of scenes is justifiable, if only on the grounds that the best way to ensure a favourable screen adaptation, whether of a play or a novel, is not to adapt the finished product but to return to the author's original concept and then rebuild it in cinematic terms. If investigated carefully, complaints that film-makers do not cleave sufficiently to the original book or play often seem to suggest that the film-maker's real failure lay in not making *enough* changes.

The performances in *Antony and Cleopatra* are variable: John Castle's Octavius is excellent and Eric Porter as Enobarbus is in compelling form; Hildegarde Neil's Cleopatra caused most of the negative critical comment. In his *Journals* Heston refers again and again to the casting of this key role and the problems that arose, even to the point where it was suggested some years later that the scenes with Cleopatra be reshot with a different actress. In fairness, he also later conceded that the part was perhaps the most difficult ever written for a woman. She 'has to be queen, bitch, mistress and child,' he once remarked.

Aside from any other issue, Shakespeare's textual references to his

Greeting John Castle in Antony and Cleopatra, *a highly personal film in concept and execution.*

heroine pose their own problems. Enobarbus tells us that 'Age cannot wither her, nor custom stale her infinite variety; other women cloy the appetites they feed, but she makes hungry where most she satisfies . . .' Of all the actresses called upon to essay the role on film (or, for that matter, on the stage) it is hard to think of any, Vivien Leigh apart, who could have come close to that build-up.

Heston's own acting in the role of Antony is good and it is tempting to speculate upon how much better he could have been had he not been involved in directing the film. On balance, however, especially given the manner in which many experienced directors have failed to bring off Shakespeare on film, it may be as well that things were done the way they were. Certainly, it was a highly creditable directing début, and had it been in anything *other* than Shakespeare he might well have been granted the acclaim which was his due.

Setting aside for the moment the matter of his involvement in the film as director, Heston's interpretation of the role of Antony is never less than interesting. As might be expected, Shakespeare's later depiction of the character is more mature than on his first appearance in *Julius Caesar*. This time, Antony displays the complex behaviour of a man of great intellectual powers and vast emotional depths who knowingly refuses to free himself from the maelstrom created by his love for Cleopatra. Heston brings to his performance a world-weary self-knowledge that offsets any demand for the logical solution, which is simply to walk away. He knows that he can do so, but he also knows that if he does he is just as surely doomed. His decision to stay, to accept his destiny, is evoked with a minimum of histrionics and for once Heston's guarded manner well suits the part he plays.

The film had mixed public reactions, doing quite well in England and even better in Japan, but ultimately its main virtue, perhaps, was that Heston had taken the plunge as director and had for now, at least, assuaged his need to bring Shakespeare to the screen.

Among the many side-effects of working in the film industry are the deals that are struck, sometimes out of nothing more than the need to make a buck. In order to persuade MGM to part with some unused footage from *Ben-Hur* which he needed for the naval battle sequences in *Antony and Cleopatra*, Heston agreed to make the film about which he later remarked that while it would earn him no kudos it would earn him money. Apart from needing the money to live on, it was also a variation upon the long-running theme of his career in which he would use movie money to subsidize his work in the theatre. On this occasion, he was using commercial movie money to help support his desire to make the kind of film he really wanted to make.

The commercial film MGM wanted him for was yet another of those jeopardy-in-the-sky stories which makes miraculous the fact that the travel industry has not gone to war with Hollywood either for frightening people half to death long before they even reach the airport or, in the case of many such films, boring them into taking another form of transport.

CHAPTER
Seven

'This is the age of the victim.'
Charlton Heston

Active as he always has been, whether preparing or making films, or working with the Screen Actors' Guild or the American Film Institute, or playing tennis at the drop of a racket, Charlton Heston has never had much time for relaxation. When he has he listens to music, his taste leaning towards the classical although his social life has occasionally found him rubbing shoulders with the likes of Peggy Lee and Duke Ellington. Another important form of hard-won relaxation is reading, mostly novels; even here his interest is partly professional. Several of his film projects have begun when he read an interesting novel, often to while away the hours on long-haul flights. *Will Penny* was one significant result of such in-flight reading, but other books he read in similar circumstances either came to nothing or, as in the case of *The Osterman Weekend* which he was considering early in 1972, eventually went elsewhere.

A continuing problem for him in selecting roles remained his physical appearance and the common response that it invoked in film-makers and moviegoers alike. As he has said, he has never matched the popular image of twentieth-century man as conveyed by, among others, Paul Newman; he appears instead to fit into other centuries, either long past or yet to come. Undeniably heroic in appearance, he was fully aware that the changes in style of movie heroes were leaving him behind. Commenting upon this in an interview with the London *Evening Standard* as early as 1961, he said, 'It's unfortunate, because we don't live in the age of heroes. This is the age of the victim.'

Some actors could cloak themselves temporarily in the personalities of victims – albeit often, as in the case of Clint Eastwood and Charles

Bronson, with built-in reserves that allow them to wreak terrible vengeance in the final moments for the injustices done them during the rest of the film. And neither were those loners who scavenged the streets of temporary urban jungles suitable roles for Heston. The physically compact generation of brilliant young actors who came to the fore in the 1970s, among them Harvey Keitel, Robert De Niro, Al Pacino and Dustin Hoffman, could roam those latterday mean streets with ease. Heston was too commanding, too seemingly dominant to have made it across the sidewalk, let alone to have merged into the squalid underbelly of the city.

Oddly enough, the one type of role which became popular in the 'seventies and which he would have suited, that of the ageing cop up against the system, seems never to have been offered. George Kennedy and William Holden played such roles in movies which followed the path signposted by the policeman-turned-novelist Joseph Wambaugh, and so too did Clint Eastwood in his other major type of the period: that of the right-wing, rule-breaking, ball-busting, pseudo-moralistic killer whose sole justification for wreaking havoc wherever he went was that he carried a badge.

But, if Heston did not don policeman's garb, he did get to wear uniform on a number of occasions in the next few years, starting with that of an airline pilot.

The film he had agreed to do for MGM as a means of extracting from them the sea-battle footage he needed for *Antony and Cleopatra* also had its origins in a novel. This was David Harper's *Hijacked*, which underwent a minor title amendment to become *Skyjacked* (1972), a film which had the dubious distinction of being banned in Australia for detailing too clearly how to hijack an airplane in flight.

Hollywood has frequently exploited the airplane-in-jeopardy as a plot for a picture. In earlier years the problem was usually fog or electrical storms or dodgy engines; later, as long-distance passenger flights became the norm, the jeopardy switched to food-poisoning or heart attacks among the crew, or metal fatigue in various parts of the airframe. The advent of the hijack proved to be a different matter, for as they increased in number and ferocity passengers could readily believe that this really could happen to them. The fact that the odds are still astronomically against the average passenger being involved in a real-life hijack is irrelevant: any airport lounge or aircraft cabin may harbour potential hijackers among the throng, and once the craft is airborne its human cargo will be entirely at their mercy.

Moviemakers in the 1970s were quick to exploit the hijack as a valuable extension to the standard plot, and although later swamped by big-budget multiple-hazard variations on the same theme, *Skyjacked* is a very creditable example. Despite the predictable and unimaginative cross-section of American life represented by the passenger list, the film maintains a reasonable degree of suspense throughout most of its running time.

Heston plays Captain Hank O'Hara, pilot of a 707, who is menaced by an unknown maniac who makes his presence on board known by scrawling a warning on the rest-room mirror. Though all the passengers are acting oddly enough to make them suspects, the field is eventually narrowed down — largely thanks to the efforts of a black musician (Roosevelt Grier), who is travelling in company with his valuable string-bass. The villain of the piece is Army Sergeant Jerome K. Weber (James Brolin), who demands that O'Hara fly to Russia. This is decidedly bad news for one passenger, US Senator Arne Lindner (Walter Pidgeon). After an Alaskan refuelling stop and various other adventures along the way, including the obligatory advance arrival of a baby whose mother (Mariette Hartley) should have known better than to travel at such a late stage of pregnancy, the craft eventually lands at its unscheduled destination. The passengers and crew disembark while O'Hara and Weber fight it out in the aircraft. O'Hara is wounded, but Weber comes to a very messy end when he is shot by Russian soldiers as he leaves the aircraft and is blown up by his own hand-grenades.

The suspense is damagingly undercut by a flashback sequence which sets up the on-off love affair between O'Hara and stewardess Angela Thacher (Yvette Mimieux), but otherwise it is all solid, workmanlike stuff. Heston's portrayal of the captain is suitably realistic despite his being filmed at ground level, and the camerawork of Harry Stradling Jr proved highly effective. (A master of outdoor filming, Stradling is a second-generation photographer, his father having worked all the way through from the silent era to such Oscar-winning films as *My Fair Lady*.)

Heston's portrayal of the airline pilot owes rather more to the popular image than to reality. There is none of the forced normalcy of a nine-to-five driver of expensive machinery which some real-life pilots suggest; neither is there the seat-of-the-pants good-ol'-boy routine of some American pilots who seem hell-bent on assuring their passengers that everything is A-OK even after the wings have fallen off. It is this airline-brochure smoothness which is perhaps the least effective element of his performance, but to a great extent it doubtless reassured those members of the audience not already put off from flying as a result of everything else they saw in the movie.

129

Edward G. Robinson sampling his room-mate's cooking in Soylent Green.

Once again, a novel formed the basis of Heston's next film. This was yet another gloomy exploration of what the future might hold. Just as in his other science-fiction adventures, mankind's future is shown to be decidedly unpleasant, and this time there is a *frisson* of strong possibility that it just might happen this way.

Set in New York in the twenty-first century, *Soylent Green* (1973) paints a grim picture of what urban life is heading towards as populations increase faster than the provision of essential services and food production. The city's population has doubled its present levels and people are everywhere, crammed into overcrowded apartments and spilling into the streets. Crime and unrest are rife, but there is also an overpowering sense of futility which imparts a defeated lethargy to almost everyone.

There is still law and order of a sort, however, and when a police detective named Thorn (Heston) is called to investigate the killing of William Simonson (Joseph Cotten), a senior executive with the Soylent Corporation, the nation's major food-producing organization, he begins to uncover the edge of a massive conspiracy. Thorn is repeatedly warned off by his own boss, Hatcher (Brock Peters), and by the local governor, Santini (Whit Bissell). He also has problems with Simonson's strangely unsuccessful bodyguard, Tab (Chuck Connors), but he persists with his enquiries, his weary task being somewhat alleviated by the ministrations of Shirl (Leigh Taylor-Young), a girl who is designated as part of the 'furniture' at Simonson's apartment.

Thorn, too, shares an apartment, in his case with an elderly police researcher, Sol Roth (Edward G. Robinson), who can still remember what real food was like and is contemptuous of the manufactured kind everyone now has to eat.

Despite the efforts of the Soylent Corporation there is seldom enough even of the manufactured food and periodically riots erupt in the city's streets. Fortunately, a new product from Simonson's company is now coming off the production line. This is a green-coloured wafer, known as Soylent Green, which is said to be a highly nutritious by-product of algae.

As Thorn continues with his enquiries it becomes apparent that Simonson has been killed at the orders of the authorities because he disapproves of certain new developments taking place at the Soylent Corporation. Meanwhile, Sol Roth and other old people who remember how things were in the past have been conducting their own investigation. Although he refuses to tell Thorn what he knows, Sol is so distressed that he decides to take advantage of another state-run enterprise. Leaving a farewell message for Thorn, Sol goes to the luxuriously appointed euthanasia centre. There, he is placed in a room and sinks into a drug-induced dream during which the scenes and sounds he most loves appear to him. Hoping to dissuade his old friend from suicide, Thorn has followed Sol, but he is too late to do more than helplessly witness his death.

Thorn now follows Sol's body as it is carried from the euthanasia centre and taken on a well-guarded journey which ends at the Soylent food-manufacturing plant. Here, Thorn discovers what it was Simonson opposed so violently that he had to be eliminated.

The green wafers emanating from the processing plant are not made from algae, for even the sea cannot provide enough nutrition for the world's billions. Soylent Green is made from processed human corpses.

The Harry Harrison novel, *Make Room! Make Room!*, on which the film is based, is a classic of the genre; the film might very well have been one, too, but the opportunity was missed owing to an inadequate script and a budget to match. This is a great pity, because the performances are generally fine with Heston giving one of his more complex interpretations. As the story opens, he is a stone-faced man of action forced into doing things he detests because the alternative would be an even worse attack upon his conscience. Yet this contrasts vividly with the warm and natural friendship he enjoys with the old man. This

131

rapport is developed so well that the scene in which he stares helplessly through the window into the room where Sol lies dying is extremely moving.

The best performance in the film comes, however, not from its star but from Edward G. Robinson.

Robinson had jibbed at the contract he was offered, which proposed that part of his fee would be paid now and part later. The old actor remarked that at his age (he was 79) deferred payments had a peculiar lack of attraction. As Heston has pointed out, despite his age and the advanced stage of his illness, Robinson was never late, never missed a call and was always ready to do his job. What Robinson did not reveal was the gravity of his illness. He knew that he was dying, and there can be little doubt that this fact brought a special texture to his performance.

By one of fate's curious quirks, Robinson's death scene happened to be scheduled so that it was shot last, and thus became an appropriately fitting valediction of the career of one of America's finest actors.

Heston's stage work continued with the role of John Proctor in Arthur Miller's *The Crucible*, which ran at the Ahmanson Theatre in Los Angeles for four weeks from 5 December 1972. Two years later he returned to his favourite Shakespeare play for a run, also in Los Angeles, in which he played opposite Vanessa Redgrave as Lady Macbeth.

Given the fact that their political stances were very nearly as far apart as it is possible to be, Heston and Miss Redgrave appear to have got on quite well, though he found her rather shy and withdrawn when she was not acting. Certainly he expressed great admiration for her professional ability. Politically, they carefully avoided conflict. He remarked in an interview with Val Hennessey for *You*, the magazine of the *Mail on Sunday*, 'Obviously I disagree with her politics – she makes Jane Fonda look like Herbert Hoover. But she never forced anything down my throat. I think she thought I was a lost cause.'

Heston had now resumed his activities with SAG. He was to remain a member of the board until May 1975 and to retain his interest long thereafter, into the 1980s. His work at the AFI continued apace and while he was Chairman the Institute announced that in celebration of the role of the movies in popular culture, 23 October 1973 would be National Film Day. In the same year a festival was promoted to feature the five most controversial films of the century, thus indicating a far from conservative view of the role of film in contemporary culture.

He was called upon yet again to testify at hearings, this time on the need for more movies to be allowed on pay-cable TV so that the funds thus generated could be ploughed back into motion-picture production. In January 1973 he was invited to be narrator in a performance of *A Lincoln Address*, a new composition by Vincent Persichetti, which was to be played by the Philadelphia Symphony Orchestra and conducted by Eugene Ormandy. However, the concert was to be attended by President Nixon and at the last moment the piece was dropped in case it were to prove an embarrassment to him.

Although generally uneasy with interviewers, Heston has regularly done the rounds of the talk-shows to help promote his movies. Barbara Walters is one with whom Heston appeared to have been even less comfortable than usual. His *Journals*, however, reveal that he manages to preserve his equilibrium during media interviews by bearing in mind Laurence Olivier's dictum: 'They none of them know fuck all, laddie.'

One off-screen chore went off happily enough. This was a visit made to the studios by the Emperor of Japan. With John Wayne also in attendance the diminutive visitor was visibly overwhelmed, shaking Heston's hand interminably while exclaiming, 'Oh, you Moses. No beard now,' before bursting into delighted laughter.

The combination of Heston's customary dedication to his work, compounded by all his other time-consuming activities, finally began to take its toll of his marriage in the mid-'seventies, when tensions sprang up between him and Lydia. The outward manifestation was in her increasingly acute migraines, which proved quite devastating. Fortunately, as time passed the Hestons were able to overcome their problems, and when Lydia later began a new career as a photographer it seems that the stability of their long-lasting marriage was restored as her health improved. One plaintive comment recorded by Heston in his *Journals* must have rung true for many: 'She hates to have me gone, but she's never healthier than when I *am*.'

Heston has always loved visiting England, and London in particular, so he was happy at the prospect of a film-making stint in 1973 which was to result in two movies instead of the one originally intended (and for which the players were contracted). However, given the circumstances, it is tempting to suspect that the producers might have had a double-bill in mind all along.

In *The Three Musketeers: the Queen's Diamonds* (1973) Heston plays the role of Cardinal Richelieu. Out to cause as much embarrassment as possible to Anne, the Queen of France (Geraldine Chaplin), who has unwisely given her valuable necklace to her lover, the Duke of Buckingham (Simon Ward), Richelieu reckons without the redoubt-

133

able quartet of D'Artagnan (Michael York) and his companions, the three Musketeers, Athos, Porthos and Aramis (Oliver Reed, Frank Finlay and Richard Chamberlain).

Earning the respect of the Musketeers by somewhat foolishly challenging them all to duels, D'Artagnan then becomes their comrade when all four have to fight off guards sent to arrest them by the Cardinal. On meeting Queen Anne through her lady-in-waiting Constance (Raquel Welch), D'Artagnan learns of her problems and undertakes to help when the absence of the necklace becomes an issue. Pursued by Richelieu's men, the quartet fight their way to the coast. D'Artagnan reaches England, recovers the necklace, replaces two stones which have been removed by the villainous Milady de Winter (Faye Dunaway) and returns in triumph to save the Queen's reputation and, thus, the throne of France. By so doing he also routs the Cardinal – and becomes a fully-fledged Musketeer.

It is all very much *Boys' Own Paper* storytelling and is paced appropriately by director Richard Lester. The film mixes farce and fights, and a general atmosphere of *bonhomie* hangs over everything and everyone. The fight scenes are effectively choreographed and look real enough, even if the participants take them much less seriously than in most sword-and-cape dramas. There is an enormous wealth of background detail, so much so that unlike many such tales this one deserves seeing more than once, for the crisp thrust of the action sequences inevitably causes the first-time viewer to overlook certain enjoyable nuances.

Made as one long film with plenty of extra takes and additional scenes, the resulting footage was sufficient to allow the producers to release two complete films, much to the annoyance of the cast who had been hired, and paid, for only one. Eventually, settlements were agreed by the lawyers and the second film, *The Four Musketeers: Milady's Revenge* (1974), duly appeared. It proved, not surprisingly, to be remarkably like the first film, although not quite so much fun. Maybe some of the left-over footage had been omitted from the first film simply because it was not quite good enough. There are also some problematical loose ends, presumably because no appropriate pieces of film were available to explain satisfactorily what eventually happened to some of the characters.

Most of the performances, especially among the bit-part players, are sound and Heston's role, while small, is effectively paced to create an impression of continuing significance. Bowed and crook-nosed, he endows Cardinal Richelieu with a suitably malevolent streak which admirably fits the slightly cardboard-cut-out nature of this and all the

Scheming with Faye Dunaway at the mad hatter's ball in The Three Musketeers.

other major roles in the two movies. He had wanted to play the role for its comic worth, but director Lester prevailed, telling him to 'play it straight. The comedy will go on around you.'

Heston was back in twentieth-century Los Angeles for his next film, a disaster movie which foreshadows an event most residents of that city fear may be just around the corner.

Earthquake (1974) centres on building-company executive Stuart Graff (Heston), who is balancing his life precariously between his unpleasant wife Remy (Ava Gardner) and his unassuming mistress Denise (Genevieve Bujold). Graff's relationships with these two women are complicated by the fact that he works for his wife's father, Sam Royce (Lorne Greene), and has earlier sent his mistress's husband off on a job during which he died in an accident. Meanwhile, a seismological institute is recording increasingly severe earth tremors but

135

displays remarkable (and, it is hoped, unrealistic) hesitation in actually telling anyone about them.

When the San Andreas Fault finally makes the shift everyone has been predicting for years, Graff finds himself balanced even more precariously than he is in his private life. Aided by a hard-nosed cop, Lew Slade (George Kennedy), who has been suspended from duty for striking a superior officer, Graff does what he can as the city and the minor characters break up all around him. He soldiers on, saving lives, hoping for the best and fighting off various oddballs, including Jodie (Marjoe Gortner), who takes his duties as an army reservist called up to preserve law and order somewhat too seriously. Finally, Graff is faced with the choice of surviving with his mistress or being swept away in the floods in what he knows will be a doomed attempt to save his wife's life. He opts for the latter and disappears into the churning waters.

Director Mark Robson handles events well. He seldom worked long enough in one genre to be typed and his screen credits are starred with numerous fine movies. He was co-editor of three of Orson Welles' films, including *Citizen Kane*; he worked with Val Lewton, eventually direct-

In Earthquake *neither Heston nor Ava Gardner had even to pretend to like each other.*

ing five movies for that master of the cheap-but-good horror tale; he directed two superb boxing films, including *Champion*; and swung easily between war stories, such as *Von Ryan's Express*, and mindless titillation, as exemplified by *Valley of the Dolls*.

The somewhat perfunctory screenplay for *Earthquake* was co-written by George Fox and Mario Puzo, whose *Godfather* novel had given him an entrée to Hollywood at the highest level, regardless of whatever qualities he might have had as a scriptwriter.

The performances in the film, as is often the case in both disaster movies and epics, are overshadowed by events. George Kennedy is sound, as is Genevieve Bujold, despite the fact that the relationship with her lover seems a trifle forced. Reunited with Ava Gardner, with whom he had had problems last time out (in *55 Days*), there was no need this time for Heston to strive for any interraction other than that called for by the script. The characters don't like one another, and that's that.

Marjoe Gortner's is an unusual case, even by Hollywood's standards. He had been a child evangelist, preaching fire and damnation on the revivalist circuit of Middle America. When he grew up, a TV documentary was made about him. This was *Marjoe* (1972), and as a result of this brief involvement with showbusiness he was tempted away from the Bible-thumping circuit into a career as an actor.

Heston's performance is rather subdued. Given the exigencies of the plot he should either be terrified out of his wits and heading for the tall timber, or a super-hero who fears nothing. Instead he opts for the midway course and attempts to give some depth to a characterization which cannot stand the weight when the rest of the film is so clearly geared to the collapse of the city rather than the more subtle disintegration of human relationships. As performances in such films go, his is creditable but by no means as strong as that which an actor of his standing might be expected to give.

The real stars of *Earthquake* are, however, the special-effects team, who certainly did an impressive job. Their miniature sets are remarkably well executed, and Philip Lathrop's photography is vivid. The added effects of 'Sensurround', a system which allowed some movie theatres to show the film complete with shaking seats, were unnecessary. Indeed, it must surely have had a decidedly negative influence on audiences, especially in California.

Heston's next film, *Airport 1975* (1974), is another airplane-in-jeopardy movie. This time, a 747 in the process of being diverted from LA to Salt Lake City has an unexpected addition to its passenger list and cargo manifest when a small private plane, flown by Scott Freeman

Preparing for take-off with Karen Black in Airport 1975.

(Dana Andrews), hits it and rips into the fuselage. The 747's pilot, Captain Stacy (Efrem Zimbalist Jr), is blinded, while various members of the crew are either killed or injured. The chief stewardess, Nancy (Karen Black), takes the controls until such time as a helicopter-borne rescue team can arrive in the vicinity.

The passengers are the usual carefully mixed crowd. They include Mrs Patroni (Susan Clark) and her young son Joe (Brian Morrison), a small-time actor named Barney (Sid Caesar), Mrs Devaney (Myrna Loy), who is an alcoholic and, by way of variation, Gloria Swanson playing herself. Least probable of all is the singer Helen Reddy as a guitar-playing nun who is even funnier, if unintentionally so, than her later counterpart in *Airplane*, which so successfully parodied this kind of movie.

The rescue mission is being handled by Joe Patroni (George Kennedy), who owns the airline and is naturally concerned that his wife and son are aboard the stricken 747. Aided by flying instructor Alan Murdock (Heston), whose concern is heightened by the fact that the stewardess now flying the aircraft is also his girlfriend, the rescue team approaches the 747 in its helicopter. An attempt is made to winch Major John Alexander (Ed Nelson) aboard, but he is killed in the attempt. Alan Murdock now tries, successfully makes the transfer and brings the crippled aircraft safely to the ground.

Jack Smight's direction is a shade turgid even if the screenplay, by Don Ingalls, was much lighter in weight than the Arthur Hailey novel, *Airport*, which had initiated this sequence of movies with the film of the same name in 1970.

Most of the actors say their predictable lines adequately enough in their brief appearances; only Karen Black has an opportunity to display much histrionic range, building into near-manic hysteria convincingly enough. She began her acting career at Northwestern University, where Charlton Heston had begun, moved on to Broadway with mixed results and then came to Hollywood for a series of small parts which only rarely used her gifts and her unusual slant-eyed presence to good effect. The exceptions included *Easy Rider* and *Five Easy Pieces*, but not until *Can She Bake a Cherry Pie?* did she get the kind of role she deserved – even if it was, unfortunately, in a film which was rather too offbeat to succeed with the public.

Heston did rather more than simply go through the motions for his role. He spent a lot of time in flying simulators, eventually taking the controls of a real 747 for long spells of mid-air filming, thus significantly adding to the long list of skills he has acquired for the movies. He makes a rather more convincing pilot than did Dean Martin in the first film in the series but, even so, cannot fully carry off the essential implausibility of his mid-air transfer.

Airport 1975 is remarkable not so much for the performances of its actors as for those of its stuntmen, and especially Joe Canutt, once again working with Heston. His mid-air work is truly spectacular and was just as dangerous as it looks.

These two films were made back-to-back, which gave Heston only a 15-hour gap between his last scenes on *Earthquake* and his first on *Airport 1975*. Quite clearly he made these for the money, but they also proved to be big commercial successes. What remains a permanent mystery about most disaster movies is why no one ever seems prepared to spend a tiny percentage of the effects budget on having someone write a better script. At least it would make the scenes in between the elements of the disaster watchable – which they almost never are.

Heston was back in the saddle for his next film, *The Last Hard Men* (1976). As lawman Sam Burgade he is pursued by Zach Provo (James Coburn), who has recently escaped from prison and now seeks vengeance on the man who sent him there. Burgade is retired, but he decides to help Marshal Noel Nye (Michael Parks) capture the outlaw. Unfortunately, the trap they set does not work and instead Provo kidnaps Burgade's daughter Susan (Barbara Hershey). Burgade follows the trail along with the Marshal and a posse which includes

Susan's boyfriend Hal Brickman (Christopher Mitchum). Provo has acquired a gang of rapacious cut-throats, most of whom have eyes for Susan. Eventually, Provo enters an Indian reservation and only Burgade and Brickman follow. Now it is Provo's turn to set a trap, which he does by letting two of his men loose on Susan. In the ensuing gun battle the outlaws are killed by Burgade and Brickman, with Provo falling to the old lawman's gun only after he has first wounded him.

This is yet another tale of a pair of ageing men of the West trying to come to terms with the changing world in which they are living out their declining years. Unfortunately, unlike some entries in this particular sub-genre, *The Last Hard Men* never quite succeeds. It is not so much that the story has been done before. What western script has not? A key problem here is that Andrew McLaglan's direction never takes a firm enough hold. A lifelong devotee of John Ford, upon whose work he consciously models his own, McLaglan has neither the judgement nor the pace of his idol, nor his ability to invest his characters with the right emotional context for their actions.

The acting of younger elements in the cast is variable. Although somewhat mannered, Barbara Hershey has always been good if shamefully under-used by Hollywood. Michael Parks seems to belong in another film, while Christopher Mitchum has neither the personality nor the skill of his father, Robert. As the two ageing hard men, both Heston and Coburn are as good as the script and direction allow them to be. If anyone had hopes that this might turn out to be another *Will Penny*, they were to be very swiftly dashed.

The crustiness with which Heston endows his character is appropriate enough, but the essentially downbeat nature of the plot, together with the fact that the two old-stagers are on opposite sides, does not give him anyone of substance to play off. Instead, he has to make do with the relatively inexperienced youngsters. Instead of developing an endearingly jokey character, as did, say, Burt Lancaster in *Cattle Annie and Little Britches*, or Robert Mitchum in *The Good Guys and the Bad Guys*, Heston ends up merely petulantly irritable and much less likeable.

Heston was back in uniform for his next film, this time as a naval commander in *Midway* (1976), centring upon the Battle of Midway (the film's alternative title) which was the turning point in the struggle between the Japanese and American navies in World War II. Much of the story told is based upon historical fact, and for the most part the film does not shirk at revealing the flaws in strategy and administration which hampered the Americans during the early stages of the war in the Pacific. All the real naval commanders are here, Nimitz, Halsey, Fletcher, Spruance (cameoed by Henry Fonda, Robert Mitchum,

Robert Webber and Glenn Ford) and others; but the main events are interspliced with the fictional tale of Captain Matt Garth (Heston), who spends part of his time in the thick of the battle and part struggling through masses of red tape to help gain the release of his son's girlfriend, one of thousands of Japanese-Americans interned following the attack on Pearl Harbor.

In a similar surprise air-attack, the Japanese bomb Midway, which is where Tom Garth (Edward Albert) has been posted. The aircraft have flown from four Japanese carriers. When the American fleet arrives three of these ships are destroyed but the fourth survives. Then Matt Garth leads an assault on the last carrier but is killed. The battle of Midway is won by the Americans and Tom Garth is reunited with his girlfriend.

The entirely unnecessary sub-plot does nothing to help the film, and the running time it occupies could have been put to better use by showing more of the Japanese side of events, as did *Tora! Tora! Tora!* when covering the earlier stages of the war in the Pacific.

Heston's performance is not as good as it could have been: he fails to flesh out a character who was badly underdrawn by the screenplay.

Given the fact that he is the principal character in a cast which includes many real-life giants of recent American military history, there appears to have been a tendency both in script and in performance to play down the role of Captain Garth. For whatever reason, the decision was unwise. As a dramatic presentation, rather than a documentary, the film needs its central fictitious core, but there is a curiously hollow feel to Garth's role. It cannot be that Heston lacks the presence to allow him to blunt even the attack of such screen heavyweights as those playing the real-life roles. Perhaps it was deference to memories which many Americans hold dear; if so, the sentiment can hardly be criticized on moral grounds but it certainly does not help the movie.

The photography commands most of the audience's attention, however, thanks to Harry Stradling Jr, here in the wide open spaces which are his milieu.

Interestingly, in his *Journals*, Heston draws attention to the fact that one of the real-life naval commanders was having problems at the time of the battle but the naval adviser to the film crew was unwilling, even 30 years on, to allow his colleague's failings to be held up to public view.

Although top-billed in his next film, Heston's role is almost a cameo and a great deal seems to happen on screen before he ever puts in an appearance.

Two-Minute Warning (1976) is another people-in-jeopardy tale. On

Taking charge of John Cassavetes and Martin Balsam before the Two-Minute Warning *gun goes off.*

this occasion, by way of a change, they are all members of the crowd gathering for a football game at the Los Angeles Coliseum. Unknown to anyone, a deranged sniper (Warren Miller) has plans for the game's visiting celebrity, the President of the United States, and has climbed to the top of one of the stadium's towers.

When the sniper is accidentally spotted by a TV camera mounted on the Goodyear blimp which is sailing over the stadium, veteran Police Captain Peter Holly (Heston) is called. Taking charge of the situation and aided by stadium manager Sam McKeever (Martin Balsam) and a SWAT team under the command of Sergeant Chris Button (John Cassavetes), Holly attempts to scale the tower, but the sniper has picked his spot well and they fail to reach him. Eventually, the President's plans are changed and his non-appearance is announced to the crowd. Naturally, the waiting sniper also hears this and starts shooting at random, wounding or killing several people drawn mostly from those individuals the camera has earlier dwelt upon. As the rest of the huge crowd panics, the SWAT team and Captain Holly manage to climb the tower, but not before the sniper has killed some of the police officers. Finally, Holly shoots the gunman.

The film works better than many stories of this type, although the necessary structure is now so well known to anyone who watches movies that there is little left to surprise or involve the viewer. There are ways to overcome the problems inherent in this kind of script, but no one seems yet to have worked them out satisfactorily.

Given the fragmentary nature of the film, the various characters who are to be at risk are set up much more effectively than is usual and there are good, if brief, appearances by David Janssen and Gena Rowlands as a pair of lovers quarrelling because he does not want to marry, Walter Pidgeon as an elderly pickpocket no longer deft enough for his job, Jack Klugman as a gambler, Mitchell Ryan as a priest, and Beau Bridges, who is giving his wife and children an enjoyable day out before breaking the news that he has lost his job. Their fleeting moments on screen are used to good effect and it is possible to care what happens to them.

Also instrumental in giving the minutiae of the film the clarity needed, but which is too often lost by less able moviemakers, is director Larry Peerce. The son of Jan Peerce, the star tenor of pre-war New York's Metropolitan Opera Company, his relatively small output of films include *Goodbye, Columbus* and *One Potato, Two Potato*, one of the best films to deal with interracial conflict and, in this case, marriage.

Heston's character in this film is inadequately shaded, something which may be accounted for by his late appearance on screen, when most of the other characters are already established. Unfortunately, this same late arrival means that he needs strong and memorably distinct qualities, but they do not materialize. The role could have been given to any second-stringer without adversely affecting the movie as a whole.

In his *Journals* Heston observes that he does not believe that all guns in private hands should be either registered or confiscated, while admitting to the prejudice which results from lifelong personal experience of gun-handling. Given that the kind of situation depicted in *Two-Minute Warning* not only can but does happen with depressing frequency in America, his view appears to be, at best, remarkably sanguine.

By now Heston was in his mid-50s, and if his last few film roles had neither tested him nor enhanced his career, they had certainly not damaged his bank account. At the time, he speculated that he might perhaps be making too many films. In fact it was not so much the quantity of his output but its quality that was most problematical. Even when a film was good, as in the case of *Soylent Green*, problems arose over the quality of its making.

Understandably aware of this, he began to look with more care at the nature of the projects he undertook. Unfortunately, as had happened so often in the past, his judgement of movies still in the planning stage remained flawed, and a few more second-rate productions were due to sail over the horizon – albeit, in one case, just beneath the surface of the ocean.

143

CHAPTER
Eight

'The minute you feel that you have given a faultless
performance is the time to get out.'
Charlton Heston

Times had changed since Charlton Heston began working in
films. Techniques had advanced enormously and a whole new breed of
cinéastes had appeared on the scene, all with a burning desire to make
movies. They too sought to make changes, throwing out old ideas and
styles, old methods and notions. Even some of the old crafts had gone,
replaced by startling technical innovations. As is always the case in
whatever field of endeavour, making it differently was not necessarily
synonymous with making it better. Part of the problem lay in the fact
that it was not just the old crafts that were dumped unceremoniously
on the waste-tip. Along with them went some of the old craftsmen.

Waiting while technicians struggled to set up a process shot, Heston
irritably remarked that were Cecil B. De Mille still around he would
have had five guys' heads on stakes for incompetence. Such impatience
is justifiable, for just as it is the actors who get all the girls, they also
collect the blame when things are seen to be wrong with the finished
film. As he remarks in his *Journals*, 'If the film fails, it's my failure, not
[that of] some sloppy crewman who can't do his job right.' Nevertheless, he could also honestly accept that sometimes the crew had a right
to be miffed, if not incompetent. It was always the actors who got most
of the rewards: glory, girls and money.

The movie that had generated his irritable comment was a submarine drama being made in Hollywood, but before that he had made
a brief appearance in another historical drama, filmed and set in
England but, thanks to the complexities of latterday film financing,
released as a Panamanian production.

The Prince and the Pauper (1977), which is based upon Mark Twain's tale, tells of a young London pickpocket, Tom Canty (Mark Lester), who bears a startling resemblance to the heir to the throne, Prince Edward (also Lester). In escaping from an angry mob, Tom clambers over a wall and finds himself face to face with King Henry VIII (Heston). Escaping the King's anger, thanks to the intervention of the Duke of Norfolk (Rex Harrison), Tom meets Edward. The two boys realize their close physical resemblance and change clothes. When discovered by courtiers, the prince, now dressed as Tom, is ejected and reunited with his 'father', John Canty (Ernest Borgnine). After various adventures, during which he is protected by Miles Hendon (Oliver Reed) and meets the outlaw known as the Ruffler (George C. Scott), the prince gradually convinces his new friends that he really is the heir to the throne.

Meanwhile, young Tom is having a hard time at the palace, where his strange behaviour convinces the court that he is insane. Nevertheless, with the old king now dead, Tom is prepared for his coronation. Miles has also run into problems with his brother Hugh (David Hemmings), who has usurped his claims to the family estate and also to Lady Edith (Raquel Welch). Miles overcomes his brother's schemes, in

Relishing another of history's larger-than-life characters in The Prince and the Pauper.

the process learning some of the problems the young prince is facing in trying to convince people that he really is who he says he is. Miles helps Prince Edward return to the palace, where he changes roles with Tom Canty just before his coronation as King Edward.

As directed by Richard Fleischer, what should have been a cheery romp through an entertaining if unlikely sixteenth-century England emerges as an uncertain shuffle from one set-piece to the next, with a cameo-role player lurking in every corner. Unlike *Two-Minute Warning*, in which the cameo players had similarly short screen time but were nevertheless able to establish effective characterizations, the many big star names here are unable to do much more than display their make-up and costumes before being hustled off to make way for the next. Much more effective is the even longer list of character actors, drawn mainly from British TV, all of whom give solid, workmanlike performances during their few minutes on the screen.

Apart from adding another of history's larger-than-life characters to his personal roll-call of performances, this film (released in some countries as *Crossed Swords*) did little for Heston's reputation with the wider audience. Most who saw this film (and here was another occasion when a Heston movie had only a limited release) were there for reasons other than his presence. In fact, limited in scope and screen time though it is, his is an interesting version of one of Great Britain's most fascinatingly complex monarchs in his last years – and one who has, understandably enough, attracted great interest among moviemakers. There is inadequate evidence here to suggest that Heston would have proved to be as convincing as many of the fine actors who have portrayed Henry VIII in the various stages of his life, but he might well have proved to be among the best at showing the king in his old age.

If this film failed to enhance Heston's reputation as an actor, then doubtless of equal, if not greater, importance was the fact that it helped his bank balance, giving him continuing freedom to look for more demanding and more interesting work in the theatre.

The submarine movie that had prompted his vexed comment about inept technicians was *Gray Lady Down* (1977), an adventure which in fact depended heavily upon technicians both on screen and off.

Captain Paul Blanchard (Heston) is commander of the submarine *Neptune*, which he is bringing back into the US Navy's base at Norfolk, Virginia, prior to his promotion. Also on board is Commander Samuelson (Ronny Cox) who will be taking over command of the submarine from Blanchard. The chief officers are all below, celebrating the hand-over of command, when the vessel, which is sailing on the

Enduring the cramped and sweaty confines of a sunken submarine with Stephen McHattie in Gray Lady Down.

surface in dense fog, collides with a freighter. The submarine sinks, touching bottom on the lip of an underwater canyon, where it becomes trapped. The submarine's officers wrangle over who is to blame for the disaster: Samuelson believes that Blanchard was guilty of grandstanding his final approach to harbour by sailing on the surface; also unhappy at the turn of events is crewman Murphy (Stephen McHattie), who was on watch at the time of the collision and considers himself to blame for what has happened.

Meanwhile, on the surface, a rescue mission commanded by Captain Bennett (Stacy Keach) gets under way. A new deep-sea rescue craft, the DSRV, is sent out, but its task, which is to couple-up to the submarine's escape hatch and allow the trapped men to transfer, is rendered impossible as the *Neptune* slides further into the canyon. With time and hope running out, the decision is made to allow an even newer, and still experimental, vessel to attempt a rescue. This is the *Snark*, which is commanded by Captain Gates (David Carradine). When the *Neptune* lists to the point where the escape hatch is covered, Blanchard risks blowing his tanks in an attempt to right the submarine. This suicidally dangerous task is undertaken by Samuelson and Murphy. Then Gates succeeds in detonating an explosive charge which removes an obstruction in the canyon and the DSRV is able to couple-up to the submarine. As the trapped men begin to transfer to safety the *Neptune* starts to slide again, but Captain Gates steers the *Snark* beneath it, thus saving the submarine and its crew at the cost of his own life.

The film is largely intent on exploiting the complex hardware used by the United States Navy, with whose collaboration the film was made. As a result, the role of the actors often dwindles to merely keeping things ticking over between rescue attempts. The tensions and squabbles, whether ashore, on the surface or beneath the sea, are mostly handled effectively. The cramped and sweaty conditions of submarines have proved useful settings for several movies, not least because the fears which must surely lodge at the back of any submariner's mind can create powerful dramatic tensions. Although little that is done and seen here is original, and has often been done to better effect, *Gray Lady Down* has some good moments – even if the self-sacrificial urges of some of the characters are inadequately explained.

Given the qualification that the behaviour of many of the characters is inexplicable, most of the cast do well with their parts but everyone plays second fiddle to the machinery. As part of his preparation for the film Heston sailed aboard a nuclear submarine, apparently enjoying his day in its claustrophobic confines. He was able to absorb some of the mannerisms of men working in these conditions but clearly, and indeed fortunately, could not expect to pick up an indication of how such men would react in a real-life sinking.

Unfortunately, tight-lipped dedication and grim awareness of the dangers which surround submariners at all times, and especially during the course of a disaster, remain merely mannerisms in Heston's performance. Little sense of the emotional turmoil suffered by men trapped in such conditions comes across. In fairness, none of his co-actors achieves as convincing a portrayal as, say, the German actors in the recent TV series *Das Boot*, a vivid representation of life, and death, below the waves.

A few years earlier Fraser Heston, now in his early twenties, had visited the far north of the American continent and had lived for a while with Indians and Eskimos in Alaska. Additionally, he had visited the high country of the Rocky Mountains and had developed a fascination for the kind of men who had first set foot in these beautiful but often forbidding regions. Now beginning to take an interest in writing for the movies, he had written a screenplay about that strange and hardy breed of nineteenth-century Americans, the mountain men.

The real-life mountain men were for the most part trappers, although some later became guides to explorers and mapmakers. They lived lives of almost unimaginable hardship amidst landscapes of monumental grandeur. That they were travelling where no white man had ever set foot, and indeed in many cases where no human being of any race had ventured, seems to have been a part of the motivation which drove them. Even so, they were not romantics, although some film-makers have chosen to depict them in this way. They were men of iron-hard will and ox-like constitution. Theirs was not so much a capacity to endure loneliness but a positive need for it. Living on whatever food they could find or kill, surviving winters of mind-numbing cold, avoiding Indians when they could and killing them (or being killed) when they could not, they, perhaps more even than those stoic endurers, the later pioneers who swarmed across the country, were the true hard men of the American frontier.

For men such as Jim Bridger (the first white man to set eyes on Salt Lake) and Hugh Glass, perhaps the worst disaster that could strike was not, in fact, a major dramatic confrontation but the simplest of accidents: a broken arm or leg could mean their facing a lonely death from hunger or exposure. Yet they too endured, opened up the West and entered American folklore as true giants of the past.

Naturally, Hollywood was attracted to such individuals but tended to concentrate upon later periods when civilization was starting to catch up. Part of the problem with the earlier breed of mountain men was the fact that they spent so much time alone. Earlier generations of moviemakers were unwilling to spend valuable screen time with only one man on camera, who therefore had no one to talk to, or make love with, or fight, or otherwise react to. Another (imagined) difficulty for film-makers was that these men were uncomfortably close to the Indian in the behaviour they were obliged to adopt in order to survive. As Hollywood had followed the tradition of earlier newspaper and maga-zine writers, and the government, in painting vivid pictures of the savagery of the Indian, by way of justifying the inhuman treatment the white man meted out, comparisons with the Indian gave rise to the suggestion that some early white Americans had chosen to live like savages. This was clearly an unacceptable pose for a movie hero.

Later film-makers, especially screenwriters and photographers, realized that a man alone could be portrayed interestingly and even excitingly. Similarly, it was gradually, if reluctantly, accepted that the supposed savage behaviour of many mountain men was not all that different from how man lived in the latterday urban jungles of his own making. Even so, few film-makers were prepared to risk going back to the first half of the nineteenth-century for their tales, preferring instead to stay closer to modern times and mix mountain men up with the classic period of the Western myth.

The 1970s saw two examples of early mountain-man movies, both good in their own way; however, both avoided showing their heroes in total isolation, and both called upon conflict with Indians for their major action sequences. The first of these two was Robert Redford's 1972 film *Jeremiah Johnson*; the second resulted from Fraser Heston's first screenplay and starred his father.

The Mountain Men (1979) is set in Wyoming in the 1830s and traces the last stages in the life of Bill Tyler (Heston), a fur-trapper. Tyler is teamed up with another trapper, Henry Frapp (Brian Keith), and Nathan Wyeth (John Glover), a businessman who sells the furs to the fashion industry in the East. During one trip the trappers run into trouble with a tribe of Blackfoot Indians led by Heavy Eagle (Stephen Macht), but Tyler rescues the chief's squaw, Running Moon (Victoria Racimo), when her life is threatened by a band of Crow Indians.

Times are changing for the fur trappers, partly owing to female fashion, which no longer dictates beaver fur. Frapp and Wyeth part company with Tyler, who is determined to soldier on – alone if necessary. But Running Moon has re-entered his life and together they head for a distant valley where beaver are still plentiful. There they encounter Heavy Eagle, who now hates all white men thanks not only to the way they are treating his lands and the animals which he needs in order to survive, but also because his people have been stricken by disease brought by the interlopers. Tyler escapes and meets up again with Frapp and two other trappers, all of whom are soon killed off by Heavy Eagle and his men. Intent on rescuing Running Moon, for whom he now feels a deep attachment, Tyler returns and finds her alone in a ravaged Indian camp. When Heavy Eagle appears he challenges the trapper to a duel, at the end of which Tyler lies dead but the Indian is shot by Running Moon.

As in the Redford film, too much attention is paid to the conflict with the Indians (in both cases the much-maligned Crows) and not enough to allowing the more intimate human relationships to develop. There

Displaying the iron-hard will of The Mountain Men.

are a number of other similarities in the two films: the flamboyant Henry Frapp and Running Moon reflect the earlier film's Will Geer as Bear Claw and Delle Bolton's Swan. Also, in both films, the scenery is the real winner. In the Heston film it is Yellowstone National Park, the Bridger-Teton and Shoshone National Forests and the area around Jackson Hole in the Rocky Mountains, which gleam attractively from the screen thanks to the superb photography of Michel Hugo.

The storyline of *The Mountain Men* has many creditable subtexts, but those that could have been most usefully employed to the ultimate

151

benefit of the picture are abandoned as the action moves on to some other sequence which, while undoubtedly attractive to the eye, does little for the mind. There is, for example, the relationship between the trapper and the Indian who eventually kills him. In many respects they are alike, ageing anachronisms in a world that is geared to changes brought about for the most trivial of reasons, in this case the demands of women's fashion. The similarity in the two men's purpose and fate is underplayed to an extent which devalues their eventual death struggle. Nevertheless, there is much that is good about the film. In this, his first screenplay, Heston's son showed that his early adventure in the screen trade, as the infant Moses in *The Ten Commandments*, had not wholly diverted him from the movies as a place in which to build a career.

The acting performances are sound, if a shade subdued (Brian Keith's rip-roaring Henry Frapp apart), as if everyone were overawed by the wilderness around them. As Bill Tyler, Heston has a role which fits closely his rough-hewn physical persona and also has echoes of Will Penny. The essential difference, however, is that Will was everyday-real and has counterparts in all times, even today. Bill Tyler and his kind were out of their time even while they lived. Heston does not succeed in conveying what made the real mountain men so very special among early American pioneers. As a result of this failure fully to explore the nature of the mountain men the film suffers. Nevertheless, although the end result could have been better it was still a decided improvement on his last few screen roles. Critically, the film was quite well received, although *Variety* accurately observed that this 'bloody wilderness pic may have trouble in finding an audience'.

For his next film, Charlton Heston entered a field which, while new to him, had provided latterday moviemakers with a seemingly endless, if often confusingly interchangeable, selection of stories.

In 1975 he had turned down a role in a film which dealt with the supernatural. Filmed as *The Omen*, with Gregory Peck in the role Heston had not wanted, the film had proved a huge commercial success and was the first of a trilogy. As such tales continued to be successful at the box-office, Heston now decided to accept a film dealing with the supernatural: this time not the advent of the Antichrist into contemporary western civilization but a favourite theme of Hollywood for decades, the return to earthly life of a long-dead Egyptian princess.

The story of *The Awakening* (1980) begins in Egypt in 1961, as archaeologist Matthew Corbeck (Heston) discovers the long-hidden tomb of Queen Kara. For reasons only hinted at, this tomb had been deliberately concealed by the ancient Egyptians. Helped by his assistant, Jane Turner (Susannah York), Corbeck breaks through into the tomb at exactly the moment that his wife Anne (Jill Townsend) is elsewhere painfully giving birth to their daughter. As excavation gets under way and a sarcophagus is lifted from the burial chamber, an over-officious representative of the government attempts to interfere with Corbeck's work but is killed in a mysterious accident. Later, angry at her husband's obsessive dedication to his work, a dedication which is not so intense that it shuts out Jane Turner, Anne returns to New York taking baby Margaret with her.

Several years elapse and Corbeck, now married to Jane, sends one of the artefacts recovered from the tomb to his daughter as a gift for her eighteenth birthday. Intrigued by the gift, a mirror, and the strange response it generates within her, Margaret (Stephanie Zimbalist) decides to travel to England where her father and Jane now live. She hopes to learn more about the ancient queen of Egypt. Corbeck tells Margaret how Queen Kara had been forced to marry her own father and had subsequently brought about his death. Kara's mummified body has now been brought to England at Corbeck's insistence following the discovery of decay. When the Egyptian archaeologist Dr Khalid (Bruce Myers) tries to stop this he dies, in an accident. Corbeck's assistant, Paul Whittier (Patrick Drury), is also against the mummy being in England and tries to persuade Corbeck to return it to Egypt. He is unsuccessful but does not press his opinions because he has become romantically involved with Margaret. This relationship is curiously one-sided, for Margaret has little interest in the young man.

Encouraged by his daughter and her growing interest in the occult beliefs of the ancient Egyptians, and in particular those which attend the legend of Queen Kara, Corbeck decides to travel to Egypt with Margaret. From the site of the tomb he removes a sealed jar containing Queen Kara's organs. He also takes away the valuable Jewel of the Seven Stars which is needed to perform a ritual designed to return Kara to life. When Jane tries to destroy Kara's organs she too dies in a mysterious accident. Corbeck is also the victim of an attack by someone seeking to steal the jar but he survives. By now, Margaret has become concerned that she is being taken over by Queen Kara's spirit and she consults a psychiatrist, Dr Richter (Ian McDiarmid), whom she later kills. Matthew Corbeck begins the ritual which will return Kara to life but realizes that when he does so Margaret will be possessed by an ancient and evil queen. He tries to halt the process by destroying the mummy, but then a huge sarcophagus falls, crushing and killing him, just as happened to Kara's father long ago. The transformation continues and the evil Queen Kara is free to live again – this time in twentieth-century London.

Based upon Bram Stoker's novel *The Jewel of the Seven Stars*, the storyline of the film is woven somewhat more densely than most films of its genre and its earlier close cousins, the 'mummy's curse' stories. In fact, this same Bram Stoker tale formed the basis of a Hammer horror flick, *Blood from the Mummy's Tomb*.

Especially interesting in potential is the intertwining of contemporary incestuous guilt complexes with the commonplace intermarriages of ancient cultures. Unfortunately, this potential is let slip by the film's makers, as if they were nervous at the direction in which such strands of the storyline might lead them. Similarly underdeveloped is the plot line which deals with the relationship between Corbeck and his assistant before she becomes his second wife. The conflict generated by the triangle of father/daughter/second wife is also allowed to escape with a few meaningful glances.

All the principals work well within the somewhat limited framework of the personas granted them by the screenplay. Apart from being a greatly gifted actress, Susannah York has a smouldering sensuality which is too often subordinated to the needs of an unimaginative character, as here, or, as in other screen roles, dissipated in barely restrained emotional hysteria. Stephanie Zimbalist is effective enough, although her relative inexperience inhibits those moments when her character's relationship with her father should steam with suppressed sexuality. Heston fares well in the film's earlier stages when masquerading as a younger man. Later, when he is playing his own age, he has to contend with some fairly heavy-handed direction and the over-dramatic needs of the plot.

More than in most of his films, Heston is here working with a cast in which all other major roles were women. His customary stiffness works well with his first wife, with whom he is supposed to have problems, but sits uneasily with his second wife and is a noticeable drawback in his relationship with his daughter, towards whom he should have demonstrated much greater warmth. Given what happens at the end of the film, Corbeck's problems with women extend even to those who have been dead for two thousand years.

Although Heston had earlier remarked that he could not have done better than Gregory Peck in *The Omen*, he probably wishes he had taken that movie instead of *The Awakening*.

The last few years of the 1970s saw no let-up in Heston's desire to use the money he made in his often less-than-impressive movies to subsidize his work in the theatre. As always, he tackled the big parts and in the winter of 1976-7 played James Tyrone in Eugene O'Neill's

Long Day's Journey into Night. He was less than wholly satisfied with his performance although the play did well, breaking house records at Los Angeles' Ahmanson Theatre. In an interview with Guy Flatley of *The New York Times* he remarked on Fredric March's performances in the play, admitting that 'if it were still possible to see [him] play James Tyrone, maybe I wouldn't be playing him now.'

At the 1978 Academy Awards ceremony Heston received the Jean Hersholt Humanitarian Award, given for distinguished service in the film industry and which recognized his visits to Vietnam.

He remained active with the American Film Institute, where he regularly rubbed shoulders with politicians who found it helped their public image to be associated with popular culture. Senators John V. Tunney and Alan Cranston were both Honorary Chairmen of the Institute, as was Tom Bradley, Mayor of Los Angeles.

Heston also became rather more deeply embroiled in political matters, one of which eventually turned rather nasty.

Uniquely American are those fringe areas where showbiz and politics meet and occasionally merge. Heston was among the many stars who attended, and entertained at, Ronald Reagan's Inaugural gala in January 1981 and soon afterwards, in May, he was appointed co-chairman of a Task Force set up by the President to study the structure of arts and humanities endowments.

It was, however, through the activities of the Screen Actors' Guild, in which he no longer held office, that Heston attracted most, and decidedly unwanted, publicity. The fact that this led eventually to threats upon his life was in stark contrast to his earlier high-profile but generally happy association with the Guild.

The problems surfaced early in 1982. One concerned the Guild's annual award made to figures within, or at one time associated with, the film industry, whose achievements warranted public acknowledgement. The award, which is given 'for outstanding achievement in fostering the finest ideals of the acting profession' had gone in the past to Bob Hope, James Stewart, Edward G. Robinson (Heston's co-star in *Soylent Green*) and Heston himself. The 1981 award was offered to Ronald Reagan, but the Guild's recently appointed public relations director, Kim Fellner, was an outspoken supporter of the American trades union movement. Believing that in making the award to the President the Guild would risk alienating the rest of the labour movement, she wrote to all board members suggesting they should intervene. The subsequent withdrawal of the offer of the award angered many, among them Charlton Heston. One of many supporters of Kim Fellner's action was the Guild's current president, Edward Asner.

It was, however, one of Asner's public statements which most agitated Heston. Although an excellent actor with many fine big-screen supporting and character roles to his credit, Asner had become best known to the public at large through his role as Lou Grant in TV's *The Mary Tyler Moore Show* and later in that show's spin-off, *Lou Grant*. Asner went on record as supporting the rebels in El Salvador and actively campaigned for funds to supply much-needed medical aid for that strife-torn country. Many Guild members took issue with Asner, partly for backing an organization against which the Administration in Washington had all but declared war, and partly because he had failed to make it clear that his public pronouncements were his privately held views and not those of the Guild.

The importance of the Guild in the overall scheme of American labour-management relations is out of all proportion to its size. With only about 50,000 members, the Screen Actors' Guild is a small union, but the AFL-CIO (an approximate American equivalent to Britain's TUC) was well aware of the publicity value attached to a union numbering many popular celebrities in its membership. The AFL-CIO confrontations with the Reagan Administration were then at a high pitch and unions needed all the favourable publicity they could get. Heston's entry into the fray allowed both press and Guild members to indulge in simplistic polarization of the issues. Edward Asner was labelled 'a Communist swine' by placard-carrying activists to the right of the Guild while Asner was reported to have tagged Heston as having a 'master-race mentality' (elsewhere amended to a more generalized comment that 'actors think of themselves as a master race').

The shadow of the 1950s red-baiting witch-hunts, which had never fully cleared from Hollywood's skies, loomed again when *Lou Grant* was dropped by CBS, despite its being one of the most highly rated of TV dramas; CBS's action triggered allegations of political censorship by sponsors.

Heston's objections to the direction in which the Guild appeared to be headed were, on the whole, pragmatic rather than political. He was concerned that instead of allowing itself to be used as a political battering-ram by the AFL-CIO the SAG board should direct its attention to such real and pressing problems as the high level of unemployment and the low average income of the Guild's members. At this time, as always, and despite having several figures in its ranks who were paid millions, Guild members held bottom place on the list of average earnings of all affiliated unions.

One of the board's current concerns to which it was addressing itself was whether or not the Guild on the west coast should merge with the much smaller Screen Extras' Guild. Here again Heston was in conflict with Asner and his supporters. Heston joined others of like mind in forming AWAG (Actors Working for an Actors' Guild). They considered that to allow extras to become members of SAG on the west coast (they are affiliated in the east) would diminish the status of the acting profession. Asner and other supporters of the merger (which included at least two of Heston's former co-stars, Joan Hackett from *Will Penny* and Jessica Walter from *Number One*), believed that the extras' guild needed the support it would get from the merger as a means of fending off the growing use of non-union labour in movies. All this, which came at a time when many other states in the Union were actively encouraging film producers to work away from California by offering substantial concessions and aid, served only to exacerbate relationships within SAG; these reached a startlingly unpleasant low point when a group calling itself the Workers' Death Squad threatened Heston's life and he had to be placed under police guard.

It was not all conflict, however, and in August 1982 Heston and Asner jointly condemned proposed legislation designed to exempt some personal managers from California state laws and union rules. This would have allowed studios, networks and independent producers to become personal managers, thus bypassing agents and leaving the artists they represented without independent protection.

But such moments of harmony were short-lived. Asner – for reasons probably incomprehensible to those Americans who harboured a paranoic fear of Communist infiltration from Latin America – pursued his genuine concern for the treatment being arbitrarily meted out south of the border by an overreacting Administration in Washington. By the end of 1983, when Asner came up for re-election, a boycott of the poll was advocated by those who opposed him. In the event, he was re-elected with a 73 per cent majority of the votes cast, although this represented only 25 per cent of eligible voters.

Apart from the issues arising from his conflicts with the board of the SAG, Heston also found himself involved in high-profile political issues when he clashed with actor Paul Newman over the nuclear freeze. Newman supported a freeze while Heston strongly opposed one. In June 1983 he addressed the National Center for Legislative Research in Washington, DC, referring in his speech to 'another actor' who had declared his support for the freeze 'by saying, "No, I haven't *read* anything about it. I don't need to. This is a gut issue." Indeed it is. But you can't think with your guts. You can, of course, think of the search for peace as a moral obligation incumbent upon every human being. Let us do that by all means.'

Also in the course of this speech, Heston vigorously stated his view that the American government could not afford to risk taking the word of the Russians on any of the issues involved. 'To put it succinctly,' he declared, 'the Soviets have violated nearly every treaty they have signed since the founding of the Soviet state in 1922.' After citing instances of this from the League of Nations through to Helsinki and the Strategic Arms Limitation Treaty, he continued, 'A nuclear freeze observed by us and broken by the Soviets would be suicidal, I think most would agree. Therefore, on the historical record, it is unnegotiable.' Later, underlining his position, he observed: 'Since almost no one will seriously defend the idea that the Soviets can be trusted to keep an agreement on their own, a freeze treaty depends on verification.' He ended his peroration by saying, 'we live – God knows we always have – in an infinitely dangerous world. We'll never get out of it alive. But while we are here, surely reason must tell us to put the infinite treasure of the peace of the world in the hands of those we love, not those we fear.'

Despite holding political views strong enough to be called to deliver such speeches as this, Heston has repeatedly refused to become actively involved in the wider political scene. Even so, it appears strikingly out of context for an actor, even one with the authority invested by his standing within the profession, to be afforded the opportunity to address such bodies and once having done so to be reported widely. As recently as July 1985 he has rejected a call to run for office as Republican candidate against Democratic Senator Alan Cranston of California, yet the suspicion remains that he is not as opposed to the idea as his repeated refusals might suggest. Having played Mark Antony in *Julius Caesar*, Heston cannot be unaware of the manner in which Caesar is eventually persuaded by his supporters to accept the crown. Equally, of course, he cannot fail to be aware of Caesar's fate at the hands of those whom he thought were his friends.

If Heston were to become seriously interested in a political future there arises the intriguing prospect of a confrontation between him and another movie star, Robert Redford, who has already tested the water for an ecologically-based campaign for political office.

If Heston entertained such thoughts as the 1980s got under way they were well hidden. He was still very much concerned with making films: one of those he had lined up was very much a Heston family affair, another was for TV, and he was also due to return to television in a mini-series, after many refusals of such work. Most important to him, he had several stage appearances before him, including the realization of a long-held ambition to appear in London's West End.

CHAPTER Nine

'Is the story about me?'
Charlton Heston

'I suppose as you get smarter you may get a little choosier – but that's presuming you get smarter.' This mildly self-deprecating remark came in a 1985 interview Heston gave to Andrew Lorenz in *The Scotsman*. Clearly aware that his choice of roles over the years had sometimes been much less than cautious, he continued, 'As I grow older there are fewer stories about the character I would play, and then fewer that would attract me. It's not that I would do only stories that are about me . . . but . . . that's the basic leading actor's question – "Is the story about me?".'

Looking back across the years since his acting début, it is hard to think of any role he has played which completely fulfils this criterion. True, there have been elements of the real Charlton Heston gleaming through some of his characters. For the most part, however, the readily evident characteristics, those of a stern, unbending pillar of rectitude, a man of unshakable integrity, a man with a dour sense of destiny, miss the real man's essential humanity. There are few signs of shyness and vulnerability, yet he is shy and vulnerable. He rarely displays self-doubt on the screen, yet that too exists. The possibility that this powerful figure of granite strength could ever crumble seems ludicrous, but such a fate can befall anyone. Only when some hint has been made that such human failings as these might exist beneath the carefully constructed shell does a Charlton Heston performance take off and offer those qualities of acting which can transform that which is workmanlike into greatness.

On those few occasions when he has shown the crumbling figure beneath the toughened exterior (*Will Penny, Number One, Major Dundee*) or the core of self-doubt hidden by layers of arrogant confidence (*El Cid, The War Lord, Khartoum*) the quality of his performance has risen dramatically. It is in such film roles as these that the moviegoer is allowed to glimpse some of the qualities which illuminate his stage performances in *Macbeth, Long Day's Journey into Night* and *A Man for All Seasons*. It is unfortunate for his international prestige as an actor (as opposed to that he holds as a 'star') that he has tended to reserve such performances for the theatre.

In the theatre his interpretations, rather than being fully developed on opening night, have evolved during the run of a play. This capacity to build and grow in a part is highly creditable, but in a screen actor it can cause problems because many film-makers are reluctant to budget time for rehearsal. How much better Heston's screen work might be if he could also benefit from the growth possible in the theatre is a matter for speculation.

In America, especially in Los Angeles, his theatrical reputation is solid yet, ironically, his cinematic following appears strongest outside America where, until recently, no one has had an opportunity to see him on stage.

Among the stage performances he gave in America in the early 1980s was one which was prompted by a visit to the theatre while he was in London filming *The Awakening*. The play was *Crucifer of Blood*, in which Heston took the role of Sherlock Holmes for a run at the Ahmanson Theatre in Los Angeles. He was anxious at first, in case it was thought too lightweight, but was persuaded that his following was such that people would come anyway and, after all the heavyweight roles he had played over the years, maybe they deserved something a little livelier.

As always, he took great care in his preparation, even to the extent of consulting a doctor to ensure he used a hypodermic needle correctly when simulating the great detective's drug habit. He could, of course, have left out references to Holmes' addiction, knowing that only those members of his audience who had read the books would be aware of the omission. Only once in the Basil Rathbone series of films is there the briefest of nods towards Holmes' use of drugs, when, in the last moment before the credits roll, Holmes cries out, 'Watson, the needle.' In the event, both audiences and actors enjoyed the play, and Heston was suitably impressive in deerstalker and cape as he brandished pipe and magnifying glass.

At the end of 1983 he was preparing yet another run of *Detective Story*, playing Denver before coming to Los Angeles for a six-week engagement early in 1984. In many respects *Detective Story*, which was so innovative in concept and construction when Sidney Kingsley first wrote it back in the 1940s, has been overtaken by the old enemy, television. The police procedural story has become commonplace and the complex *mise-en-scène* of such shows as *Hill Street Blues* has changed audiences' perceptions of how police-station interiors look and sound and how the denizens of such places conduct themselves. Nevertheless, what was startling to audiences when the play was first produced is still interesting and surprisingly undated almost 40 years on. However, some of the substance of the plot has proved to be less durable.

The obsession of detective Jim McLeod (Heston) with tracking down an abortionist (Donald Hotton in this production) carries much less impact than was once the case, although the revelation that Jim's wife (Mariette Hartley here playing the role so often played by Lydia) had once used the abortionist's services still carries a punch. The steadfast righteousness of McLeod might today be better overlaid with a patina of weary cynicism, but his commitment is still believable. Others in the supporting cast for this production included an excellent John Schuck as McLeod's partner Brodie (Schuck has almost made a career out of playing assistants to detectives, including a long-running role in the popular TV series *McMillan and Wife*) and the two small-time crooks were well played by Charles Whiteside as Lewis and Keith Carradine as Charlie.

Not surprisingly, given his familiarity with the play, Heston seriously considered this for his London theatrical début when such a possibility was first mooted, but by the time the problems of bringing over an American production complete with cast had been cleared away he had changed his mind.

In his non-acting commitments, Heston remained very busy, but still found time for sketching, a pastime at which he has become highly proficient, which is not really surprising given his determination to be good at everything he does. He was still exercising constantly, usually by playing tennis, and was also on the move for other reasons. In 1982 he visited Mexico City as a State Department observer at the UNESCO World Conference on Cultural Policies. Writing of this first visit in *American Film*, he was pithily critical of the fact that the purpose of the conference remained obscure while the delegates, who numbered well over 2,000, appeared to be drawn largely from non-artistic milieux. Observing that the French Minister of Culture chose the occasion to launch a blistering attack on American film, Heston countered with a plea for non-interference by politicians. Only three years later, the Americans, wearying of their Aunt Sally role in UNESCO, bowed out, pulling the British along behind them.

Heston's hopes for non-intervention in the arts and entertainment by politicians mirrored his view on censorship, which he also stressed in interviews around this same time. However distressing it might be to some that things were done and said in film, on stage and on television that might be better left undone or unsaid, external imposition of censorship was a potentially crippling alternative.

Not that Heston was unaware of the potential of film in matters political, observing, 'That prescient political genius Lenin identified film in 1921 as the crucial weapon in the war of ideas it has since become.' Thus far, he has not chosen to exploit a film of his own for such purposes, despite the indubitable undercurrent of morality pervading much of his work.

As to the accumulation of material which related to his work, in 1983 he decided to hand over to the Theater Arts Library at the University of California in Los Angeles his personal archive of scripts, sketches, books and memorabilia. This material is now stored in the Charlton Heston room at the Library.

Heston's reluctance to appear in television drama was beginning to evaporate, and he took a role in the thriller *Chiefs* (screened in Britain in 1983 as *Once Upon a Murder*).

Beginning in 1924, this story is set in the small town of Delano, Georgia. Actively promoted by Senator Hugh Holmes (Heston), the town is growing and now has its own police department. Among the local citizens who apply for the job of police chief are World War I veteran Foxy Funderburke (Keith Carradine) and Will Henry Lee (Wayne Rogers). Much to the resentment of Foxy, Will Henry gets the job but fails to solve the mysterious death of a young boy who is found beaten to death. When another similar death is reported, it all becomes too much for the chief, who was formerly only a farmer, but he continues to record his observations of the case. Will Henry's task is not helped by the obstructive behaviour of County Sheriff Skeeter Willis (Paul Sorvino), who thrives on bribery and corruption and is determined to maintain appearances that the community is calm and law-abiding. Will Henry is killed by one of Delano's poor blacks, who mistakenly believes that he is suspected of a serious crime.

After the end of World War II, the town's growth continues apace and police officer Sonny Butts (Brad Davis) tries to discover more about the old killings and continuing disappearances of young boys, often hitch-hikers passing through. Then he too mysteriously disappears, along with his motorbike.

By the early 1960s Billy Lee (Stephen Collins), Will Henry's son, is running for governor, enthusiastically backed by Senator Holmes, and together the two men persuade the city council to appoint ex-military policeman Tyler Watts (Billy Dee Williams) police chief, concealing until it is too late the fact that Watts is black. The appointment causes great consternation and generates hatred from the prejudiced Skeeter Willis. Watts has his own secrets, for he grew up in Delano and it was his father who killed Will Henry Lee many years before.

Watts also takes a professional interest in the deaths and disappearances of the young boys and, using a combination of modern statistical procedures and the old files his predecessors had kept, the new police chief gradually begins to uncover the truth about those long-ago killings.

Struggling against the disbelief of the townspeople, and in some instances their outright refusal to help, he finally obtains permission to search Foxy Funderburke's lonely cabin. At first nothing is found, but then Watts stumbles over something protruding from the ground and as he turns to look, Foxy grabs a gun and tries to kill him. Foxy is overpowered by other policemen and Watts uncovers what is buried there. It is the motorbike belonging to the missing police officer. They now start to dig vigorously and soon uncover not only the body of the dead cop but also the bodies of more than 20 young boys, all victims of Foxy's sadistic sexual attacks.

Screened as a mini-series which runs for more than five hours, *Chiefs* is partially successful but loses ground through the flat style of directing and photography so beloved of TV companies and through failing to maintain any suspense regarding the identity of the murderer, even in the early stages.

Performances are varied, with Wayne Rogers making a mark as the indigent farmer who makes an honest if hopeless – and ultimately fatal – attempt at becoming a policeman. Paul Sorvino is suitably egregious as the corrupt Sheriff and would be almost too blackly villainous were it not for the fact that the real-life behaviour of some Southern cops has now been shown on factual television programmes so often. Keith Carradine, as the deranged killer, does well when acting the young man but does not age too well. The manner in which he broods lovingly over the uniform he bought to wear as police chief and has kept in pristine condition, wearing it only when he sexually assaults, then beats and kills his victims, is chillingly convincing. As the state senator, Heston's role is peripheral despite his top billing. In the early episodes he is filmed gauzily to help him look younger, while later he looks just as patriarchal as state senators, especially Southern state senators, are supposed to look (according to the movies). As an acting performance, however, he breaks no new ground and appears to be well aware that the best roles are all being played by others.

Before *Chiefs*, Heston had made a major big-screen film that has never, despite an out-of-competition screening at the 1982 Cannes Film Festival, been widely shown.

Mother Lode (1981) was very much a Heston family affair. Fraser Heston had spent time in the desert regions of the south-western states and had also visited parts of Canada. Having picked up many fascinating tales of gold-miners in these remote and still unpopulated regions, he wrote a screenplay and spent some years trying to raise the finance needed to produce it. The central role was well-suited to his father, provided that he could for once be persuaded to play the part of a downright villain. It was only later that the idea arose that it might also be a movie Heston would want to direct. Eventually that matter too was settled, but money was still a problem. Peter Snell, who had produced *Antony and Cleopatra* for Heston, was called in and eventually the finance was raised, mostly in Canada and some of it through individual public subscription. By this time Fraser Heston was resident in Canada, having married a Canadian girl in 1980. Now Marilyn Heston was the unit publicist and Lydia came up to shoot location stills.

Set in British Columbia, the story follows the dangerous adventure of Jean Dupré (Nick Mancusco) and Andrea Spaulding (Kim Basinger), who fly north in search of their friend, a pilot who has disappeared. Along the way they land on a river when their dilapidated yellow seaplane develops engine trouble. They make the acquaintance of Elijah (John Marley), a wise-cracking old Indian fisherman who fixes the engine. Further north still, they reach the lake they believe their friend was headed for in his search for gold, but when they land their aircraft capsizes. After scrambling ashore they manage to bring out most of their equipment. That night, they hear the sound of bagpipes playing in the forest and go to investigate. They find a cabin inhabited by a half-crazy, heavily-bearded Scotsman, Silas McGee (Heston). Although Jean tries to keep their interest in gold a secret, Andrea lets it slip. The old miner tells them that the mine he is working nearby contains only silver. He takes them into the tunnel, warning them of the dangers, especially a vertical shaft several hundred feet deep.

That night, Andrea encounters a man in the woods but escapes when he tries to grab her. The next day Jean finds traces of gold in the river. When they later discover the sunken wreck of their friend's airplane they are convinced that McGee is not only lying to them but is dangerous. Jean sneaks into the tunnel and discovers that no real mining is taking place and the face is ore-free mud. Andrea joins him, having learned that McGee had a demented twin brother he claims is now dead. Then an explosion occurs; both are trapped, but in different parts of the tunnel. With an effort, Jean, who is nearest the entrance, manages to get out while Andrea is helped free through an air-shaft by a strange, shaggily-bearded figure. Jean goes to the cabin and someone attacks him in the dark; he retaliates and strikes a fatal blow, but runs without discovering whom he has killed.

Determined now to find the secret of the mine, and believing Andrea to be dead, Jean collects ropes from his sunken seaplane and descends the vertical shaft. When his anchor-point gives way he falls into the water at the bottom of the shaft, where he finds his friend's decomposing body. Jean then finds another tunnel and eventually reaches the place where McGee really has been mining, but once again there is only mud. From there another vertical shaft leads upwards, this one complete with a ladder. Climbing up, he opens a trapdoor and is back in the cabin. McGee is waiting for him, and lying on the floor where he fell when Jean struck him in the dark is the dead body of McGee's twin brother.

McGee now admits he is searching for gold, the mother lode of all the gold found in these parts over the past hundred years, but he is fighting a losing battle to reach it before the river water breaks through and floods the mine. He offers Jean a deal but the young man refuses and leaves. Then Andrea reappears to tell Jean that Ian McGee saved her from the mine. Jean is no longer sure which brother is the crazier, or even which he has killed. They start to pack, so that they can return to civilization, but then Andrea disappears again. McGee has taken her into the mine. Jean follows with his shotgun and this time he finds gold, masses of it, but the river breaks through and the flood carries him away from the treasure. Meanwhile, McGee drags Andrea back up the shaft to his cabin and attacks her with an axe. Jean comes up the shaft in time to shoot McGee, who falls to the bottom of the shaft.

Jean and Andrea go to the river bank as Elijah comes along in his powered canoe to bear them away from the scene.

Some of the elements of the storyline are a mite hazy at times, although much of the woolliness is probably intentional. Certain mysteries are unexplained, others are revealed too soon, among them the fact that the missing pilot is shown being killed right at the start of the film.

Mother Lode is very much an outdoor (and underground) adventure movie, completely different to anything Heston has done before. Shot in a region located to the north of Vancouver, the Stikine river and

Cassiar mountains scenery is beautifully evoked by cameraman Richard Leiterman. The action sequences are well-staged (Joe Canutt was again second unit director), and however improbable much of the storyline might be Heston, as director, keeps things zipping along. Nick Mancusco is effective in his role although his shifts of motivation, as gold fever rises then subsides, are a little hard to accept. Kim Basinger is a shade disappointing after her performance in Robert Redford's most recent film, *The Natural*. In fairness, her part is insubstantial and her character inadequately developed. John Marley as the crusty old Indian has all the best lines in the script and clearly relishes a change from all the years playing newspapermen or villainous members of the Mob.

Also obviously relishing a change of pace is Charlton Heston, who seizes his first opportunity to play a villain without a single redeeming feature and even manages a commendable Scottish accent. This time, the task of directing and starring in a film presents fewer problems than it had with *Antony and Cleopatra*, notwithstanding one moment when the pressure caused him to dry (forget a line of dialogue) for what may well have been the first and only time in his career.

Although set in the present, the role of McGee is comparable to that of Bill Tyler in *The Mountain Men* and Heston's acting performance, while suitably unpleasant, might well have been better for dispensing with beard, straggling hair and accent and thus coming nearer to a realistic portrayal of a present-day man driven mad by the ancient curse of gold fever. In the event, he turns in a character-actor's performance in a second-string role when he could, without detriment to the second half of the film, have taken command.

The Hestons decided against putting *Mother Lode* in the hands of a major distributor, so the film has therefore not had a full national theatrical release in America. Instead they have allowed it to emerge in one part of the country at a time. Plans to approach each international market on a similarly piecemeal basis have restricted overseas showings although the film's sale into the home video market will allow more people to see it in due course.

Similarly limited in its exposure to the public was another Heston adventure film, shot in Kenya as a TV movie but also released on the home video market.

Nairobi (1984) begins when Rick Cahill (John Savage), a former Green Beret who lives and works as a game warden in Kenya, is sent to another region of the country with orders to stop the poachers who are killing elephant and rhinoceros herds for their ivory. Before he leaves, however, he attends his mother's funeral. Also at the graveside is Rick's former girlfriend Anne Malone (Maud Adams), but there is no sign of his father, who is now Anne's lover. Eventually Lee Cahill (Heston) arrives, and it is soon obvious that little love is lost between father and son. Rick heads for the region where the poachers are working, an area where Lee, a former big-game hunter, lives and works as a guide for tourists.

While Lee and his camp manager Simon (John Rhys-Davies) entertain camera-mad Arthur Gardner (Shane Rimmer) and his man-mad wife Helen (Connie Booth), Rick runs into trouble when he is shot at by poachers. Crash-landing near his father, he survives and is soon on the poacher's trail again, this time in a truck. He finds and captures two poachers and hands them over to the Masai, who are reputed to have no mercy on such men.

Although Lee now has a somewhat less demanding pair of tourists under his wing, he is having trouble with Simon, who keeps disappearing from camp. Anne has also joined Lee and, aware that she has not fully got over her affair with his son, he asks her to marry him. She is not yet ready for such a step, however.

Rick is in trouble again, this time having the tyres of his truck shot out; after walking back to Lee's camp, he asks for the loan of another truck. Lee agrees but, having just found Anne in Rick's arms, he decides that he will go with his son. After they have left, Simon quietly leaves the camp too. Rick and Lee eventually find a party of four poachers, and while they are sneaking up on them they see Simon drive up and greet the men. It is clear that they are in Simon's pay. When the shooting starts, the poachers are killed but Simon makes a run for it. Rick and Lee pursue him on foot, and Lee takes him prisoner. Losing his temper with the man, whom he has known for fifteen years, Lee beats Simon up but is himself stabbed in the stomach.

Rick forces Simon to help carry his wounded father to the truck and they return to the Masai village, where Simon is handed over to the men while the women treat Lee's wound. Rick sends for Anne and an aeroplane to fly his father out to hospital.

As Rick and Anne prepare to drive Lee to the landing site, the Masai let Simon free and then begin to hunt him down.

At the landing site, Lee asks to be lifted from the truck. 'This is a good place,' he says, 'the place where the world began.' Then he dies, leaving Rick and Anne together.

Nairobi has the same problems most TV movies have to suffer: flat direction and unimaginative photography. There is also an intrusive element of predictability in the screenplay. Years ago, Hollywood had the problem of not knowing how to handle its male stars when they reached an age at which the moviemakers felt reluctant to let them get the girl. Feature film-makers have overcome that problem but TV seems stuck with it.

As Simon, John Rhys-Davies turns in another of his many solid performances of untrustworthy individuals, usually seen only on British TV. Here, he manages to imbue his character with depths which are not really present in the script. At odds with the acting style of everyone else in the movie is John Savage, who seems to have adopted some of the least convincing elements of the Method.

As the ageing hunter, Heston is generally good and in the scene in which he declares his love for the much younger woman he is far more impressive than in almost any comparable scene he has played over the years. All the old guards are down for once and the scene works well enough to have allowed the writer to permit an ending reflecting present-day attitudes towards relationships between young women and older men.

Despite the film's failings it was unfortunate that, twice in a row, Heston had made movies which could not be seen by the wider cinema audience. Consequently, many might have thought that during the first half of the 1980s he had dropped out of active film-making.

Politically, late 1984 saw Heston still being pursued by Californian Republicans, who considered him a good bet to stand against Alan Cranston in the 1986 Senate elections. Heston was as cautious as he had been in the past, remarking to the *Los Angeles Times*, 'I do not belong to either party. I have always been an independent,' adding that, in any case, 'I don't want to give up acting.' The problem of people taking him for what he purported to be on screen, as opposed to what he was in real life, emerged as he asserted, not for the first time, that 'every known actor is followed by the length and shadow of his roles, not his politics.'

It was in 1985 that Heston finally achieved a long-standing ambition to act on the stage of London's West End.

The plans had been under consideration for some time but needed reciprocal arrangements if the production was to be predominantly American rather than a largely British production into which the big star was dropped. Eventually, a deal was worked out which took Alan Bates to the Ahmanson Theatre in Los Angeles with John Osborne's *A Patriot for Me* and Heston to England with Herman Wouk's *The Caine Mutiny Court-Martial*.

Based on Wouk's own Pulitzer Prize-winning novel, the play, unlike the 1954 film which starred Humphrey Bogart, is set in a court room (save for a short closing scene at a party) with the events at sea being described but not seen. During World War II, Lt. Stephen Maryk (John Corey) is court-martialled for actions he took at sea during a typhoon. Claiming that the ship's captain, Lt. Commander Philip

As indestructible as a mountainside, before the collapse in The Caine Mutiny Court-Martial.

Francis Queeg (Heston), lost his ability to command, Maryk, urged on by the bitter Lt. Thomas Keefer (William Wright), replaced the ship's commander.

Now on trial for mutiny, Maryk is defended by Lt. Barney Greenwald (Ben Cross), who has his own problems – not the least of which is resisting the anti-Semitism of many of his fellow officers. As Greenwald's only hope of securing the release of his client is to attack his accuser, he goes after Queeg with terrier-like determination. Although in many ways reluctant in his task, Greenwald succeeds in making the first crack in Queeg's seemingly impervious shell. But that small breach in the defences is enough and, slowly at first, then with a rush, all Queeg's latent paranoia pours out in a baleful recitation of the wrongs, real and imagined, visited upon him by the uncaring volunteer naval oficers with whom he was surrounded at sea. In a closing scene, as the outcome of the trial is celebrated, Greenwald can at last make clear what he really thinks to his client, that it is men like Queeg that are winning the war, and, in destroying him, they are guilty of destroying a valuable part of themselves.

The acting performances in the production were all good, with moments of true excellence created by a cast which mixed well-known faces with others that were virtually unknown to British theatre audiences. Among the supporting actors were John Schuck and Lee Patterson, the Canadian actor who worked extensively in British films in the 1950s. As Greenwald, Ben Cross added another excellent performance to a growing list of stage and screen successes.

As Queeg, Heston's performance began as it should have, with the captain appearing as sturdily indestructible as a mountainside. His disintegration, first when the tiny hole was needled through by Greenwald, then the slow but inexorable slide as his facade slipped away, was a remarkable piece of acting. As the *Sunday Times* critic wrote, 'he present[ed] a chilling portrait of spiritual ruin.' A member of the cast made a similar comment, referring to the broken Queeg as a majestic ruin.

The audition of Jonathan Hartman, who was cast as a Lt. Commander on the court-martial board, undoubtedly reminded Heston of his own struggling days back in New York in the late 1940s. Hartman bluffed his way in and would not leave until he had been heard. His persistence paid off and the resulting experience proved invaluable. All of Heston's careful attention to detail, his meticulousness and punctuality (which he insisted was matched by everyone else) were present, but so too was a consistent courteousness which began as each candidate was auditioned and continued throughout the run of the play. Yet, busy as he always was, no detail was too unimportant to be overlooked, even to the point of advising Hartman on his make-up complete with personal demonstration. Also persistent was Heston's watchfulness as director. When not on the stage (and Queeg is only on stage for two long scenes), he could be seen by members of the cast, white shirt gleaming hugely in the dark, observing them from the wings or from a discreet box or the back of the stalls. The results of these inspections were that fine points of detail were drawn to the attention of the cast, thus making possible a continuous refinement of the production all the way through its out-of-town tryouts (in Brighton, Bath and Manchester) and through its run at the Queen's Theatre in the West End. Sometimes, however, the off-stage observations were made to enable Heston to sketch his fellow actors as they worked.

And he was forever working on his own performance – adding, changing, improving. One particular piece of business, the near fall as Queeg pushes himself to his feet as he prepares to leave the court room for the last time, was gradually perfected until no one in the suddenly shocked audience doubted that the momentary unbalancing of Queeg's chair was anything other than accidental.

During the run of *Caine* in London, Lydia Heston went into hospital with back trouble, but once the play was over and Heston's work permit neared expiry they returned to Los Angeles, where Heston had plans to stage the play at the Henry Fonda Theatre.

Very much a public figure, Heston in London was a little like Moses and the Red Sea with crowds and traffic parting in delighted waves as he walked to the theatre. He also attended a function in Leicester Square to mark British Film Year. There, in company with John Mills, Anna Neagle, Omar Sharif and Alan Bates, he recorded his handprints in cement, thus beginning a smaller-scale version of the pavement attraction at Mann's (formerly Grauman's) Chinese Theatre on Hollywood Boulevard in Los Angeles.

Back in Hollywood, the best offers were being made neither for big-screen movies nor, of course, for stage work, but for television. *Chiefs* had been a TV mini-series and *Nairobi* began life as a TV movie, but the offer he now received was one of a very different order. It was also one which must have struck hard against his artistic sensibilities, to say nothing of his concern over the quality of his scripts, but the fee offered was nothing short of awesome.

The result of the offer he could not bring himself to refuse was Heston's entry into American soap opera: not just any old soap, however, but supersuds at their most soporifically sumptuous.

C H A P T E R
Ten

'. . . don't screw up.'
Charlton Heston

For any actor who has consistently expressed concern over the
quality of the scripts he has worked with over the years, Heston's
decision to enter the deep end of American soap opera seems at first
glance to be rather odd.

This is not to suggest that the scripts for such shows *cannot* have
quality, despite the vast quantity needed for the level of output. Some
scripts are good, a few excellent, but, unfortunately, many show signs
of haste and, worse, an inadequate grasp of the fundamentals of
screenwriting. There are other problems, too: storylines may sometimes tend towards a confusing woolliness, while repetition is the
greatest bane of a producer's life. As for the acting, this is neither better
nor worse but just as variable as in all other areas of the profession. It is
the fact that there is so much of it, and hence proportionately so much
that is less than adequate, that throws an unflattering light on those
individual actors who have learned their trade in schools less demanding than that of the live theatre.

Precisely what it is about soap operas that attracts, and keeps,
audiences, often for many years at a stretch, is not a subject for this
book. Many thousands of words have already been written on the
subject, and doubtless many more will follow. Students on both sides of
the Atlantic have even taken the soaps as a subject for their university
theses. Nevertheless, now that Charlton Heston has entered soap
opera, some comments may be appropriate, at least on those areas in
which he is now working.

In comparison with the daytime soaps, of which there is, usually, one
hour-long episode a day, five days a week, all year round, the weekly

soaps are produced at a slightly less frantic pace, and, because they have an evening or even weekend slot, they attract greater advertising revenue and, hence, enjoy bigger budgets. To present-day non-American audiences, the best-known American soaps are *Dallas* and *Dynasty*.

In *Dynasty* most of the elements which go to make countless other soaps are present alongside much better than average production values, and it is tempting to suspect that it is this aspect of the series which has overcome the undoubted failings it has in all other departments. That the scripts seldom sparkle as much as the stars' costumes is not unique to *Dynasty*: it is merely exaggerated here. It cannot be that writers so often laboriously explain in great detail those things that can be more readily said in a word, or even a glance, because they are wholly inept (Alexis has been heard to remark, for example, on having something 'flown in from Paris – by air!' and to refer to 'a mutual friend – of both of us'). It must be conceded that the scriptwriters do what they do the way they do it in order to meet certain requirements of the form: that these requirements appear to be based upon an unflattering assessment of the audience's intelligence and attention span is, at best, an unfortunate reflection of television's corporate attitudes towards the public in most things; that the public at large probably gets the television it deserves is an even worse reflection of contemporary society.

The repetitiveness of much soap opera is clearly displayed in *Dynasty* as season after season rolls by during which business deals, family infighting, revelation of secrets (many of which involve one or another member of the cast discovering a long-lost, and hitherto unmentioned, relative), follow one upon the other in a manner which is curiously uninvolving. It is one such family connection which has allowed the Carrington family, which forms the centre of the saga, to throw up a hitherto fleetingly mentioned counterpart, not to say cloned, family of relations, the Colbys of California.

The head of this family is Jason Colby, in which role Charlton Heston made his first appearance in *Dynasty* for a few episodes in order to establish the connections before the spin-off series could take flight. The fact that within Heston's first few minutes on screen it was declared that his character was suffering from some unnamed terminal illness is not important. Death in *Dynasty* and its kind is not especially permanent. Characters come back from the dead with alarming regularity, albeit frequently personified by an entirely different actor where a predecessor has had the misfortune really to die (or argue too much about his contract).

In his few establishing episodes of *Dynasty*, Heston's main screen conflict came with the character of Blake Carrington, the role played by John Forsythe, with whom Heston had worked in the theatre thirty years ago. Also established in these episodes was the character of Constance, Jason Colby's sister. In giving this role to Barbara Stanwyck, the series' producers guaranteed that Heston would be working with at least one actor whose dedicated professionalism is a match for his own.

Just what he thinks of the scripts is a matter for conjecture, but a comment made in an interview with *The Observer*'s Michael Pye by British actress Stephanie Beacham, who plays Jason Colby's wife Sable, suggests that there may be trouble ahead: 'Costumes and hair before script – you can tell what really matters here,' she remarked.

Heston has long been embroiled in battles, not of his own making, to gain a measure of the critical attention he deserves. Now he is involved in a struggle not for critical ratings but for Nielsen ratings. As 1986 progressed, *Dynasty II: The Colbys*, after a bad start, was showing signs of improvement. If it does not make the grade, Heston's status in the acting community is unlikely to suffer unduly, but, equally, his standing will not shield him from the swift sword of the unhappy sponsor. Even though the threat of fatal illness was removed, some other means to an untimely end can always be invoked by the scriptwriter.

If the worst happens, he can console himself with the thought of the money, reportedly $100,000 for each episode (news of which apparently greatly aggravated Joan Collins, who plays Alexis Carrington), which will help to subsidize several more important ventures.

It would be grossly unfair to judge Charlton Heston's attitude towards his career on the basis of his decision to accept the role of Jason Colby. Regardless of the quality of his material in soap opera, matched as it has been by some ill-judged roles in the past, Heston brings to it a high degree of professionalism. He is, rightly, proud of his attitude towards his work. Interviewed by Paul Rosenfield for the *Los Angeles Times* he observed, 'I'm saying I'm a professional and good, at minimum. If things get better than that, swell. But first comes this: you don't screw up, period.'

Let us hope that the role of Jason Colby, the latest in a series of choices he has made in which the money offered has been a major factor, will bring him the freedom to continue to play in the theatre those roles which truly test him as an actor.

What those theatrical roles will be is a matter for speculation. Obviously, he has not yet done with either Sir Thomas More or

Macbeth, and he must surely dream that now the barrier to working in England has been broken he might play them in London, or, in the case of *Macbeth*, at Stratford. To do so now will need a considerable degree of commitment, not least to overcoming those critics whose armoury of cynical invective has been reinforced by his decision to accept the Colby role. There can be no doubt that he has that commitment.

Additionally, he has the capacity and the talent. If there is a touch of fear it is understandable but can be dismissed, if not readily, by reflection on a line of Shakespeare's he must have spoken times without number when Macbeth dismisses his fear of Macduff: 'That I may tell pale-hearted fear it lies, and sleep in spite of thunder.'

But *A Man for All Seasons* and *Macbeth* are by no means the only possibilities. He once declared his willingness to play in *King Lear* in a supporting role to Orson Welles. Now Welles is dead, and it can no longer be far from Heston's mind to essay not the supporting role but the lead.

Throughout his working life he has played men older than himself. At 17 he was Peer Gynt; he was President Jackson, young and old, when he was 30; and he played Moses, from youth to extreme age, when only 33. Compared with such physical transformations, playing King Lear now that he is in his early 60s would be relatively simple. But, of course, there is more to playing a role than looking the right age. Over 30 years ago, interviewed by the *Los Angeles Times*, he remarked of Shakespearean roles that an actor has to grow into them at progressive stages in his life. 'You can play Mark Antony at an earlier age than Brutus . . . and then Macbeth at a still later age, while naturally King Lear can come as the culmination of your maturity.'

The maturity needed is not merely that of the actor but also that of the man: Heston must commit himself totally to the emotional self-revelation that has illuminated some of his stage roles while flickering only intermittently during his film career. In those moments, amidst the excitement and clamour of his epic roles, and those other films in which cities shook and disaster threatened, when warmth and subtlety gleamed in spite of the thunder all around him, he has shown that he can reveal the essence of the qualities needed to encompass fully so great a role.

What remains is for him to discover within himself the self-confidence, which would surely not be misplaced, that he can do it.

If he is to play Lear at some future time it will be, quite simply, the ultimate test for an actor who has said, 'Shakespeare spells complete-ness to me in the opportunities that he affords an actor through his lifetime.'

Obviously, there must be many more big-screen roles he would like to play, and a recent revival of interest in one tried and tested motion-picture form could well be a sign for the future. As Charles Champlin of the *Los Angeles Times* commented recently, Heston, 'like many of us, wishes for the return of the western that neither remythologizes nor demythologizes but that only celebrates again a uniquely American experience.' As Hollywood has now returned, somewhat hesitantly perhaps, to the western movie, it may be that Heston could reinforce the impression generated by his role as Will Penny, and create a truly great character who will live on as long as there are movies, and certainly long after the Carringtons and Colbys have faded from memory.

The epic presence with which Charlton Heston has been physically endowed has caused him problems in the past, and the passage of time has done little to erode that image. Indeed, the ruined majesty of his appearance at the end of *The Caine Mutiny Court-Martial* suggests an artistic enhancement rather than a detraction. Yet, like it or not, while he and careful students of his work will remember him for his stage appearances and for such film roles as Andrew Jackson, Mike Vargas, Amos Dundee, Chrysagon, General Gordon, Ron Catlan, Mark Antony and Will Penny, he will be remembered by the great mass of the movie-going public for Moses and Ben-Hur. Evidently, and understandably, this irritates him, but considering the lifestyle he has enjoyed and the fame and the acclamation which follow him wherever he goes, it cannot have been too big a price to pay.

There remain, still, the frequently recurring hints of a political career. As time passes the likelihood of this must surely diminish although, given recent precedents, a transfer from the film studio to the political arena can never be entirely ruled out.

If he should enter politics without capping his career with the culminating role of King Lear it would be sad, for this would leave unresolved a final assessment of his ability as an actor – which requires much more evidence than is offered by his numerous film roles.

Judged by his stage career, especially his Macbeth and Thomas More, but without Lear, the best that can be said is, perhaps, a paraphrase of a review of one of his films: he is not quite a great actor, but he is touched with the quality of greatness.

Even at that, when Charlton Heston goes he will leave quite a hole in the history of popular cinema.

Hard to believe from this recent picture but the Hestons have now been married for more than 40 years.

BIBLIOGRAPHY

Anderegg, Michael A., *William Wyler* (Boston: Twayne, 1979)

Basinger, Jeanine, *Anthony Mann* (Boston: Twayne, 1979)

Baxter, John, *King Vidor* (New York: Monarch Press, 1976)

Butler, Terence, *Crucified Heroes: the Films of Sam Peckinpah* (London: Gordon Fraser, 1979)

Chandler, Charlotte, *Hello, I Must Be Going: Groucho and His Friends* (London: Sphere, 1980)

De Mille, Cecil B., *Autobiography* (London: W.H. Allen, 1960)

Druxman, Michael B., *Charlton Heston* (New York: Pyramid, 1976)

Elley, Derek, *The Epic Film: Myth and History* (London: Routledge & Kegan Paul, 1984)

Essoe, Gabe and Lee, Raymond, *De Mille: the Man and His Pictures* (Cranbury, N.J.: A.S. Barnes, 1970)

Funt, Marilyn, *Are You Anybody?* (New York: Dial Press, 1979)

Harrison, Rex, *Rex* (London: Macmillan, 1974)

Heston, Charlton, *The Actor's Life: Journals 1956–76* (London: Allen Lane, 1979)

Heston, Charlton, 'The Face At the Cutting Room Door', *American Film*, September 1984

Heston, Charlton, 'The Peace Movement: Nuclear Freeze', *Vital Speeches of the Day*, 15 October 1983

Higham, Charles, *The Films of Orson Welles* (Los Angeles: University of California Press, 1970)

Kaminsky, Stuart M., *Coop* (New York: St Martin's Press, 1980)

Madsen, Axel, *William Wyler* (New York: W.H. Allen, 1974)

Wallis, Hal B., and Higham, Charles, *Starmaker* (New York: Macmillan, 1980)

In addition to books, I have referred to various newspaper and magazine articles, most of which are specified in the text. I would, however, like to make special mention of the *Los Angeles Times, Monthly Film Bulletin, The New York Times, Plays & Players, Variety.*

FILMOGRAPHY

PEER GYNT
(Amateur)

1942
85 mins./16mm silent b & w

Director: David Bradley. *Producer*: David Bradley

Screenplay: David Bradley from Henrik Ibsen's play

Photographer: David Bradley

Leading players: Charlton Heston as Peer Gynt; Kathryne Elfstrom as Solveig; Betty Barton as Ingrid; Rose Andrews as Anitra.

(Later re-released with narration by Francis X. Bushman and music by Edvard Grieg.)

JULIUS CAESAR
(Amateur)

1949
90 mins./b & w

Director: David Bradley. *Producer*: David Bradley

Screenplay: David Bradley from William Shakespeare's play

Photographer: David Bradley

Leading players: Charlton Heston as Mark Antony; Frederick Roscoe as Decius Brutus.

DARK CITY
Paramount

1950
97 mins./b & w

Director: William Dieterle. *Producer*: Hal Wallis.

Screenplay: John Meredyth Lucas, Larry Marcus and others

Photographer: Victor Milner. *Music*: Franz Waxman

Leading players: Charlton Heston as Danny Haley; Lizabeth Scott as Fran; Viveca Lindfors as Victoria Winant; Jack Webb as Augie; Dean Jagger as Captain Garvey.

THE GREATEST SHOW ON EARTH

1952

Paramount

154 mins./Technicolor

Director: Cecil B. De Mille. *Producer*: Cecil B. De Mille

Screenplay: Fredric M. Frank, Barré Lyndon and Theodore St John

Photographer: George Barnes. *Music*: Victor Young

Leading players: Charlton Heston as Brad Braden; Betty Hutton as Holly; Cornel Wilde as Sebastian; Gloria Grahame as Angel; James Stewart as Buttons; Dorothy Lamour as Phyllis; Lyle Bettger as Klaus.

THE SAVAGE

1952

Paramount

95 mins./Technicolor

Dirctor: George Marshall. *Producer*: Mel Epstein

Screenplay: Sydney Boehm from L.L. Foreman's novel

Photographer: John F. Seitz. *Music*: Paul Sawtell

Leading players: Charlton Heston as Warbonnet/Jim Aherne; Susan Morrow as Tally Hathersall; Joan Taylor as Luta.

RUBY GENTRY

1953

TCF

82 mins./b & w

Director: King Vidor. *Producers*: King Vidor and Joseph Bernhard

Screenplay: Silvia Richards

Photographer: Russell Harlan. *Music*: Heinz Roemheld

Leading players: Charlton Heston as Boake Tackman; Jennifer Jones as Ruby Gentry; Karl Malden as Jim Gentry.

PONY EXPRESS

1953

Paramount

101 mins./Technicolor

Director: Jerry Hopper. *Producer*: Nat Holt

Screenplay: Charles Marquis Warren

Photographer: Ray Rennahan. *Music*: Paul Sawtell

Leading players: Charlton Heston as Buffalo Bill Cody; Forrest Tucker as Wild Bill Hickok; Rhonda Fleming as Evelyn Hastings; Jan Sterling as Denny Russell.

THE PRESIDENT'S LADY

1953

TCF

96 mins./b & w

Director: Henry Levin. *Producer*: Sol C. Siegel

Screenplay: John Patrick from Irving Stone's novel

Photographer: Leo Tover. *Music*: Alfred Newman

Leading players: Charlton Heston as Andrew Jackson; Susan Hayward as Rachel Jackson.

ARROWHEAD
1953
Paramount
105 mins./3-D and Technicolor

Director: Charles Marquis Warren. *Producer*: Nat Holt

Screenplay: Charles Marquis Warren from W.R. Burnett's novel

Photographer: Ray Rennahan. *Music*: Paul Sawtell

Leading players: Charlton Heston as Ed Bannon; Jack Palance as Toriano; Brian Keith as Captain North.

BAD FOR EACH OTHER
1953
Columbia
83 mins./b & w

Director: Irving Rapper. *Producer*: William Fadiman

Screenplay: Irving Wallace and Horace McCoy from McCoy's novel

Photographer: Franz Planer. *Music*: Mischa Bakaleinikoff

Leading players: Charlton Heston as Tom Owen; Lizabeth Scott as Helen Curtis.

THE NAKED JUNGLE
1954
Paramount
95 mins./Technicolor

Director: Byron Haskin. *Producer*: George Pal

Screenplay: Philip Yordan and Ranald MacDougall from Carl Stephenson's story *Leiningen Versus the Ants*

Photographer: Ernest Laszlo. *Music*: Daniele Amfitheatrof

Leading players: Charlton Heston as Christopher Leiningen; Eleanor Parker as Joanna Leiningen.

SECRET OF THE INCAS
1954
Paramount
101 mins./Technicolor

Director: Jerry Hopper. *Producer*: Mel Epstein

Screenplay: Ranald MacDougall and Sydney Boehm

Photographer: Lionel Lindon. *Music*: David Butolph

Leading players: Charlton Heston as Harry Steele; Robert Young as Dr Stanley Moorehead; Nichole Maurey as Elena Antonescu; Thomas Mitchell as Ed Morgan.

LUCY GALLANT
1955
Paramount
104 mins./Technicolor

Director: Robert Parrish. *Producers*: William H. Pine and William C. Thomas

Screenplay: John Lee Mahin and Winston Miller from Margaret Cousins' novel *The Life of Lucy Gallant*

Photographer: Lionel Lindon. *Music*: Van Cleve

Leading players: Charlton Heston as Casey Cole; Jane Wyman as Lucy Gallant; Thelma Ritter as Molly Besseman; William Demarest as Charley Madden; Claire Trevor as Lady Macbeth.

THE FAR HORIZONS
Paramount

1955
107 mins./Technicolor

Director: Rudolph Maté. *Producers*: William H. Pine and William C. Thomas

Screenplay: Winston Miller and Edmund H. North from Della Gould Emmons' novel *Sacajawea of the Shoshones*

Photographer: Daniel L. Fapp. *Music*: Hans Salter

Leading players: Charlton Heston as William Clark; Fred MacMurray as Merriwether Lewis; Donna Reed as Sacajawea; Alan Reed as Charbonneau; Barbara Hale as Julia Hancock.

THE PRIVATE WAR OF MAJOR BENSON
Universal

1955
105 mins./Technicolor

Director: Jerry Hopper. *Producer*: Howard Pine

Screenplay: William Roberts and Richard Alan Simmons

Photographer: Harold Lipstein. *Music*: Joseph Gershenson

Leading players: Charlton Heston as Bernard Benson; Julie Adams as Kay Lambert.

THE TEN COMMANDMENTS
Paramount

1956
219 mins./Technicolor

Director: Cecil B. De Mille. *Producer*: Cecil B. De Mille

Screenplay: Aeneas Mackenzie, Jesse L. Lasky Jr, Jack Garris and Fredric M. Frank

Photographer: Loyal Griggs. *Music*: Elmer Bernstein

Leading players: Charlton Heston as Moses; Yul Brynner as Rameses; Anne Baxter as Nefertiri; Edward G. Robinson as Dathan; Sir Cedric Hardwicke as Sethi; Vincent Price as Baka; John Derek as Joshua; Yvonne De Carlo as Sephora.

THREE VIOLENT PEOPLE
Paramount

1957
98 mins./Technicolor

Director: Rudolph Maté. *Producer*: Hugh Brown

Screenplay: James Edward Grant

Photographer: Loyal Griggs. *Music*: Walter Scharf

Leading players: Charlton Heston as Colt Saunders; Anne Baxter as Lorna Hunter; Gilbert Roland as Innocencio; Tom Tryon as Cinch Saunders; Bruce Bennett as Harrison.

TOUCH OF EVIL
Universal

1958
95 mins./b & w

Director: Orson Welles. *Producer*: Albert Zugsmith

Screenplay: Orson Welles from Whit Masterson's novel *Badge of Evil*

Photographer: Russell Metty. *Music*: Henry Mancini

Leading players: Charlton Heston as Mike Vargas; Orson Welles as Hank Quinlan; Janet Leigh as Susan Vargas; Joseph Calleia as Pete Menzies; Akim Tamiroff as Uncle Joe Grandi and cameos by Marlene Dietrich, Joseph Cotten, Zsa Zsa Gabor.

THE BIG COUNTRY

United Artists

1958
165 mins./Technicolor

Director: William Wyler. *Producers*: William Wyler and Gregory Peck

Screenplay: James R. Webb, Sy Bartlett and Robert Wilder from David Hamilton's novel

Photographer: Franz Planer. *Music*: Jerome Moross

Leading players: Charlton Heston as Steve Leech; Gregory Peck as James McKay; Burl Ives as Rufus Hannassey; Charles Bickford as Major Terrill; Carroll Baker as Patricia Terrill; Jean Simmons as Julie Maragon

THE BUCCANEER

Paramount

1958
120 mins./Technicolor

Director: Anthony Quinn. *Producer*: Henry Wilcoxon

Screenplay: Jesse L. Lasky Jr and Berenice Mosk

Photographer: Loyal Griggs. *Music*: Elmer Bernstein

Leading players: Charlton Heston as Andrew Jackson; Yul Brynner as Jean Lafitte; Claire Bloom as Bonnie Brown; Inger Stevens as Annette Claiborne; E.G. Marshall as Governor Claiborne; Charles Boyer as Dominique You.

BEN-HUR

MGM

1959
217 mins./Technicolor

Director: William Wyler. *Producer*: Sam Zimbalist

Second Unit Directors: Andrew Marton and Yakima Canutt

Screenplay: Karl Tunberg from Lew Wallace's novel

Photographer: Robert L. Surtees. *Music*: Miklós Rózsa

Leading players: Charlton Heston as Judah Ben-Hur; Stephen Boyd as Messala; Hugh Griffith as Sheik Ilderim; Jack Hawkins as Quintus Arrius; Haya Harareet as Esther; Martha Scott as Miriam; Cathy O'Donnell as Tirzah.

THE WRECK OF THE MARY DEARE

MGM

1959
104 mins./Metrocolor

Director: Michael Anderson. *Producer*: Julian C. Blaustein

Screenplay: Eric Ambler from Hammond Innes's novel

Photographers: Joseph Ruttenberg and Freddy Young. *Music*: George Duning

Leading players: Charlton Heston as John Sands; Gary Cooper as Gideon Patch.

EL CID

Allied Artists

1961
184 mins./Color

Director: Anthony Mann. *Producer*: Samuel Bronston

Screenplay: Philip Yordan and Fredric M. Frank

Photographer: Robert Krasker. *Music*: Miklós Rózsa

Leading players: Charlton Heston as Rodrigo Diaz; Sophia Loren as Chimene; John Fraser as Alfonso; Gary Raymond as Sancho; Herbert Lom as Ben Yussuf.

THE PIGEON THAT TOOK ROME
1962

Paramount
101 mins./b & w

Director: Melville Shavelson. *Producer*: Melville Shavelson

Screenplay: Melville Shavelson from Donald Downes' novel *The Easter Dinner*

Photographer: Daniel Fapp. *Music*: Alessandro Cicognini

Leading players: Charlton Heston as Paul MacDougall; Harry Guardino as Joseph Contini; Elsa Martinelli as Antonella Massimo; Brian Donlevy as Colonel Harrington.

55 DAYS AT PEKING
1963

Allied Artists
154 mins./Color

Directors: Nicholas Ray and Andrew Marton. *Producer*: Samuel Bronston

Screenplay: Philip Yordan and Bernard Gordon

Photographers: Jack Hildyard and Manuel Berenguer. *Music*: Dmitri Tiomkin

Leading players: Charlton Heston as Matt Lewis; David Niven as Sir Arthur Robertson; Ava Gardner as Natalie Ivanoff; Robert Helpmann as Prince Tuan; John Ireland as Sergeant Harry; Flora Robson as Dowager Empress Tzu Hsi; Leo Genn as Jung Lu.

DIAMOND HEAD
1963

Columbia
106 mins./Eastmancolor

Director: Guy Green. *Producer*: Jerry Bresler

Screenplay: Marguerite Roberts from Peter Gilman's novel

Photographer: Sam Leavitt. *Music*: Johnny Williams

Leading players: Charlton Heston as Richard Howland; Yvette Mimieux as Sloan Howland; George Chakiris as Dean Kahana; James Darren as Paul Kahana; France Nuyen as Mei Chen.

THE GREATEST STORY EVER TOLD
1965

United Artists
225 mins./Technicolor

Director: George Stevens. *Producer*: George Stevens

Screenplay: George Stevens and James Lee Barrett

Photographers: William C. Mellor and Loyal Griggs. *Music*: Alfred Newman

Leading players: Max von Sydow as Jesus; Dorothy Maguire as Mary; Robert Loggia as Joseph; Charlton Heston as John the Baptist (cameo). Other cameos by David Hedison, David McCallum, Sidney Poitier, Telly Savalas, Van Heflin, Pat Boone, Sal Mineo, Shelley Winters, Donald Pleasence, John Wayne.

THE AGONY AND THE ECSTASY
1965

TCF
139 mins./DeLuxe Color

Director: Carol Reed. *Producer*: Carol Reed

Screenplay: Philip Dunne from Irving Stone's novel

Photographer: Leon Shamroy. *Music*: Alex North

Leading players: Charlton Heston as Michelangelo; Rex Harrison as Pope Julius II; Diane Cilento as Contessina de' Medici; Harry Andrews as Bramante.

MAJOR DUNDEE
Columbia

1965
134 mins./Eastmancolor

Director: Sam Peckinpah. *Producer*: Jerry Bresler

Screenplay: Harry Julian Fink, Oscar Saul and Sam Peckinpah

Photographer: Sam Leavitt. *Music*: Daniele Amfitheatrof and Ned Washington

Leading players: Charlton Heston as Amos Dundee; Richard Harris as Ben Tyreen; James Coburn as Sam Potts; Senta Berger as Teresa Santiago; Warren Oates as O.W. Hadley.

THE WAR LORD
Universal

1965
122 mins./Technicolor

Director: Franklin J. Schaffner. *Producer*: Walter Seltzer

Screenplay: John Collier and Millard Kaufman from Leslie Stevens' play *The Lovers*.

Photographer: Russell Metty. *Music*: Jerome Moross

Leading players: Charlton Heston as Chrysagon; Rosemary Forsythe as Bronwyn; Richard Boone as Bors; Guy Stockwell as Draco.

KHARTOUM
United Artists

1966
128 mins./Technicolor

Director: Basil Dearden. *Producer*: Julian C. Blaustein

Screenplay: Robert Ardrey

Photographers: Edward Scaife and Harry Waxman. *Music*: Frank Cordell

Leading players: Charlton Heston as General Charles Gordon; Laurence Olivier as the Mahdi; Ralph Richardson as William Gladstone; Richard Johnson as Colonel J. D. H. Stewart.

PLANET OF THE APES
TCF

1968
119 mins./DeLuxe Color

Director: Franklin J. Schaffner. *Producer*: Arthur P. Jacobs

Screenplay: Rod Serling and Michael Wilson from Pierre Boulle's novel *Monkey Planet*

Photographer: Leon Shamroy. *Music*: Jerry Goldsmith

Leading players: Charlton Heston as George Taylor; Roddy McDowell as Cornelius; Kim Hunter as Zira.

COUNTERPOINT
Universal

1968
107 mins./Technicolor

Director: Ralph Nelson. *Producer*: Dick Berg

Screenplay: James Lee and Joel Oliansky from Alan Sillitoe's novel *The General*

Photographer: Russell Metty. *Music*: Bronislau Kaper

Leading players: Charlton Heston as Lionel Evans; Maximilian Schell as General Schiller; Anton Diffring as Colonel Arndt.

WILL PENNY   1968
Paramount   108 mins./Technicolor

Director: Tom Gries. *Producers*: Fred Engel and Walter Seltzer

Screenplay: Tom Gries from his own novel

Photographer: Lucien Ballard. *Music*: David Raskin

Leading players: Charlton Heston as Will; Joan Hackett as Catherine Allen; Donald Pleasence as Preacher Quint; Ben Johnson as Alex; Anthony Zerbe as Dutchy; Lee Majors as Blue.

NUMBER ONE (aka: THE PRO)   1969
United Artists   105 mins./Color

Director: Tom Gries. *Producer*: Walter Seltzer

Screenplay: David Moessinger

Photographer: Michel Hugo. *Music*: Dominic Frontière

Leading players: Charlton Heston as Ron Catlan; Jessica Walter as Julie Catlan; Bruce Dern as Richie Fowler; Diana Muldaur as Ann Marley.

JULIUS CAESAR   1970
American International   116 mins./Technicolor

Director: Stuart Burge. *Producer*: Peter Snell

Screenplay: Robert Furnival from William Shakespeare's play

Photographer: Ken Higgins. *Music*: Michael Lewis

Leading players: Charlton Heston as Mark Antony; Jason Robards as Brutus; John Gielgud as Julius Caesar; Richard Johnson as Cassius; Robert Vaughn as Casca; Diana Rigg as Portia.

THE HAWAIIANS   1970
United Artists   132 mins./DeLuxe Color

Director: Tom Gries. *Producer*: Walter Mirisch

Screenplay: James R. Webb from part of James Michener's novel *Hawaii*

Photographers: Philip Lathrop and Lucien Ballard. *Music*: Henry Mancini

Leading players: Charlton Heston as Whip Hoxworth; Tina Chen as Nyuk Tsin; Geraldine Chaplin as Purity Hoxworth; Alec McCowan as Micah Hale.

BENEATH THE PLANET OF THE APES   1970
TCF   94 mins./DeLuxe Color

Director: Ted Post. *Producer*: Arthur P. Jacobs

Screenplay: Paul Dehn and Mort Abrahams

Photographer: Milton Krasner. *Music*: Leonard Rosenman

Leading players: Charlton Heston as George Taylor; James Franciscus as Brent; Kim Hunter as Zira.

(Scenes with Charlton Heston were also used as flashbacks in the 1971 film *Escape from the Planet of the Apes*.)

THE OMEGA MAN
Columbia-Warner

1971
98 mins./Technicolor

Director: Boris Sagal. *Producer*: Walter Seltzer

Screenplay: John William Corrington and Joyce H. Corrington from Richard Matheson's novel *I Am Legend*

Photographer: Russell Metty. *Music*: Ron Grainer

Leading players: Charlton Heston as Robert Neville; Anthony Zerbe as Matthias; Rosalind Cash as Lisa.

CALL OF THE WILD
MGM-EMI

1972
105 mins./Eastman Color

Director: Ken Annakin. *Producer*: Harry Alan Towers

Screenplay: Peter Welbeck (Harry Alan Towers), Wyn Wells, Peter Yeldman from Jack London's novel

Photographer: John Cabrera. *Music*: Carlo Rustichelli

Leading players: Charlton Heston as John Thornton; Michèle Mercier as Calliope Laurent; Raimund Harmstorf as Pete; George Eastman as Black Burton.

SKYJACKED
MGM

1972
101 mins./Metrocolor

Director: John Guillermin. *Producer*: Walter Seltzer

Screenplay: Stanley R. Greenberg from David Harper's novel *Hijacked*

Photographer: Harry Stradling Jr. *Music*: Perry Botkin

Leading players: Charlton Heston as Hank O'Hara; Yvette Mimieux as Angela Thacher; James Brolin as Jerome K. Weber; Walter Pidgeon as Arne Lindner; Jeanne Crain as Clara Shaw.

ANTONY AND CLEOPATRA
Rank

1972
160 mins./Technicolor

Director: Charlton Heston. *Producer*: Peter Snell

Screenplay: Charlton Heston from William Shakespeare's play

Photographer: Rafael Pacheco. *Music*: John Scott

Leading players: Charlton Heston as Mark Antony; Hildegarde Neil as Cleopatra; Eric Porter as Enobarbus; John Castle as Octavius Caesar.

SOYLENT GREEN
MGM-EMI

1973

97 mins./Metrocolor

Director: Richard Fleischer. *Producers*: Walter Seltzer and Russell Thacher

Screenplay: Stanley R. Greenberg from Harry Harrison's novel *Make Room! Make Room!*

Photographer: Richard H. Kline. *Music*: Fred Myrow

Leading players: Charlton Heston as Thorn; Edward G. Robinson as Sol Roth; Chuck Connors as Tab Fielding; Leigh Taylor-Young as Shirl.

THE THREE MUSKETEERS: The Queen's Diamonds
TCF

1973

107 mins./Technicolor

Director: Richard Lester. *Producer*: Alexander Salkind

Screenplay: George MacDonald Fraser from Alexander Dumas' novel

Photographer: David Watkin. *Music*: Michel Legrand

Leading players: Charlton Heston as Cardinal Richelieu; Michael York as D'Artagnan; Oliver Reed as Athos; Frank Finlay as Porthos; Richard Chamberlain as Aramis; Faye Dunaway as Milady de Winter.

AIRPORT 1975
Universal

1974

107 mins./Technicolor

Director: Jack Smight. *Producer*: William Frye

Screenplay: Don Ingalls inspired by Arthur Hailey's novel *Airport*

Photographer: Philip Lathrop. *Music*: John Cacavas

Leading players: Charlton Heston as Alan Murdock; Karen Black as Nancy; George Kennedy as Patroni; Susan Clark as Mrs Patroni; Efrem Zimbalist Jr as Captain Stacy; Dana Andrews as Scott Freeman.

EARTHQUAKE
Universal

1974

123 mins./Technicolor

Director: Mark Robson. *Producer*: Mark Robson

Screenplay: George Fox and Mario Puzo

Photographer: Philip Lathrop. *Music*: John Williams

Leading players: Charlton Heston as Stuart Graff; Ava Gardner as Remy Graff; George Kennedy as Lew; Genevieve Bujold as Denise Mitchell.

THE FOUR MUSKETEERS: Milady's Revenge
TCF

1975

107 mins./Technicolor

Director: Richard Lester. *Producer*: Alexander Salkind

Screenplay: George MacDonald Fraser from Alexander Dumas' novel *The Three Musketeers*

Photographer: David Watkin. *Music*: Lalo Schiffren

Leading players: Charlton Heston as Cardinal Richelieu; Michael York as D'Artagnan; Oliver Reed as Athos; Frank Finlay as Porthos; Richard Chamberlain as Aramis; Faye Dunaway as Milady de Winter.

THE LAST HARD MEN
TCF   1976   97 mins./DeLuxe Color

Director: Andrew V. McLaglen. *Producers*: Walter Seltzer and Russell Thacher

Screenplay: Guerdon Trueblood from Brian Garfield's novel *Gun Down*

Photographer: Duke Callaghan. *Music*: Jerry Goldsmith

Leading players: Charlton Heston as Sam Burgade; James Coburn as Zach Provo; Barbara Hershey as Susan Burgade; Michael Parks as Noel Nye; Christopher Mitchum as Hal Brickman.

MIDWAY (aka: THE BATTLE OF MIDWAY)
Universal   1976   131 mins./Technicolor

Director: Jack Smight. *Producer*: Walter Mirisch

Screenplay: Donald S. Sanford

Photographer: Harry Stradling Jr. *Music*: John Williams

Leading players: Charlton Heston as Matt Garth; Henry Fonda as Admiral Nimitz; James Coburn as Captain Maddox; Glenn Ford as Rear Admiral Spruance; Robert Mitchum as Admiral Halsey; Cliff Robertson as Comm. Jessop; Robert Webber as Rear Admiral Fletcher; Robert Wagner as Lt. Comm. Blake.

TWO-MINUTE WARNING
Universal   1976   115 mins./Technicolor

Director: Larry Peerce. *Producer*: Edward S. Feldman

Screenplay: Edward Hume from George La Fountaine's novel

Photographer: Gerald Hirschfeld. *Music*: Charles Fox

Leading players: Charlton Heston as Peter Holly; John Cassavetes as Chris Button; Martin Balsam as Sam McKeever; Gena Rowlands as Janet; David Janssen as Steve.

THE PRINCE AND THE PAUPER (aka: CROSSED SWORDS)
TCF   1977   121 mins./Technicolor

Director: Richard Fleischer. *Producer*: Pierre Spengler

Screenplay: George MacDonald Fraser from Mark Twain's story

Photographer: Jack Cardiff. *Music*: Maurice Jarre

Leading players: Charlton Heston as Henry VIII; Rex Harrison as Duke of Norfolk; Mark Lester as Tom Canty/Prince Edward; Oliver Reed as Miles Hendon; Raquel Welch as Edith; George C. Scott as the Ruffler; Ernest Borgnine as John Canty; David Hemmings as Hugh Hendon.

GRAY LADY DOWN
Universal   1977   111 mins./Technicolor

Director: David Greene. *Producer*: Walter Mirisch

Screenplay: James Whittaker, Howard Sackler from David Lavallee's novel *Event 1000*

Photographer: Stevan Larner. *Music*: Jerry Fielding

Leading players: Charlton Heston as Paul Blanchard; David Carradine as Captain Gates; Stephen McHattie as Murphy; Stacy Keach as Captain Bennett; Rosemary Forsythe as Vickie.

THE MOUNTAIN MEN   1979
Columbia-EMI-Warner   105 mins./Metrocolor

Director: Richard Lang. *Producers*: Martin Shafer and Andrew Scheinman

Screenplay: Fraser Clarke Heston

Photographer: Michel Hugo. *Music*: Michel Legrand

Leading players: Charlton Heston as Bill Tyler; Brian Keith as Henry Frapp; Victoria Racimo as Running Moon; Stephen Macht as Heavy Eagle.

THE AWAKENING   1980
Columbia-EMI-Warner   105 mins./Technicolor

Director: Mike Newell. *Producer*: Robert Solo

Screenplay: Allan Scott, Chris Bryant and Clive Exton from Bram Stoker's novel *The Jewel of the Seven Stars*

Photographer: Jack Cardiff. *Music*: Claude Bolling

Leading players: Charlton Heston as Matthew Corbeck; Susannah York as Jane Turner; Stephanie Zimbalist as Margaret Corbeck.

MOTHER LODE   1981
Agamemnon   106 mins./Colour

Director: Charlton Heston. *Producer*: Fraser Clarke Heston

Screenplay: Fraser Clarke Heston

Photographer: Richard Leiterman. *Music*: Ken Wannburg

Leading players: Charlton Heston as Silas and Ian McGee; Nick Mancusco as Jean Dupré; Kim Basinger as Andrea Spaulding; John Marley as Elijah.

NAIROBI   1984
Robert Halmi Inc.   90 mins./Technicolor

Director: Marvin J. Chomsky. *Producer*: Robert Halmi

Screenplay: David Epstein

Photographer: Ronnie Taylor. *Music*: Charles Gross

Leading players: Charlton Heston as Lee Cahill; John Savage as Rick Cahill, John Rhys-Davies as Simon; Maud Adams as Anne Malone; Connie Booth as Helen Gardner; Shane Rimmer as Arthur Gardner; Thomas Baptiste as Nbomba.

I N D E X

Note: page numbers in italic indicate illustrations

192